The Velvet Book
    The Comforter is the Velvet Voice.
    The soft voice that Elijah heard.
    The voice that crieth out in the streets.
    Velvet is comfortable.

Isaiah 40:1-3

1Comfort ye, comfort ye my people, saith your God.

2Speak ye comfortably to Jerusalem, and cry unto her, that her warfare is accomplished, that her iniquity is pardoned: for she hath received of the LORD'S hand double for all her sins.

3The voice of him that crieth in the wilderness, "Prepare ye the way of the LORD, make straight in the desert a highway for our God."

CONTENTS

PART ONE

1. Purpose — 3
2. The Way of the Fisherman — 10
3. Four Pillars of the Fisherman — 12
4. The Fisherman's Tale of Jonah — 22
5. Dominion Over All — 25
6. The Voice of Domination — 33
7. Controlling the Light — 39
8. Presented as a Servant — 47
9. Heart's Desire — 55
10. Dominion Through Order — 63
11. Plot Armor — 72
12. Continual Sacrifice — 77

PART TWO

13. The Luxurious Calling — 83
14. Gifts and Abilities — 91
15. Synergy — 100
16. On Point — 106
17. Fishermen Certification Levels — 111
18. Temptation is the Test — 119
19. Find Peace Before the Furnace — 125
20. Deceptor — 129
21. Be the Process — 134
22. Without a List You're Listless — 137
23. Loose Ends — 144
24. Intermedium — 152
25. Appendix — 156

PART ONE

1
PURPOSE

1 Samuel 12:23-24
*23Moreover as for me, God forbid that I should sin against the LORD in ceasing to pray for you: but **I will teach you the good and the right way:***
*24**Only fear the LORD, and serve him in truth with all your heart**: for consider how great things he hath done for you.*

I am only an aspiring servant of the Father on the same walk and journey as you. I only know these trials and observations because I have gone through many of them, and I am still going through some of them now. This is my spiritual autobiography. Compiled here are the ways and methods that have worked for me throughout my life. Along this journey, I have become familiar with what I believe is the voice of the Most High. This Voice has saved my life countless times and guides me in all matters; even matters that many may see as trivial or simple but in the long-term are quite important. I identify this voice as the Holy Spirit, but at the same time, it may not be the Holy Spirit. It may be my spirit which is in contact with the Holy Spirit. This contact only exists for those with a spirit that is after the heart of the Most High. It exists for someone that is willing to do what is commanded of them.

> *1 Samuel 13:13-14*
> *13 And Samuel said to Saul, Thou hast done foolishly: thou hast not kept the commandment of the LORD thy God, which he **commanded** thee: for now would the LORD have established thy kingdom upon Israel for ever.*
> *14 But now thy kingdom shall not continue: the LORD hath sought him **a man after his own heart**, and the LORD hath commanded him to be captain over his people, **because thou hast not kept** **that** which the LORD commanded thee.*

The commandment that Saul refused to obey was not one of the 613 commandments originally given by Moses and the Levites. This was a command from the Most High given to Samuel to give to Saul to slay all of the Amalekites. I am mentioning this because many people believe that the Most High is done talking to them, whether that be through a prophet or through the Spirit. I can certify through my experiences that He is not done speaking. Yes, He speaks through the Word that is your Bible, but He also speaks through the Spirit. Saul disobeying this command that wasn't in the written law was still considered a sin.

This is the starting concept of the book for people that are walking in "the truth" or that can identify their lineage or ancient ancestors and their descendants in the Bible. If you have not identified yourself or your people in the Bible, I advise you to research and seek to find out who you and your people are/were to the best of your ability. The Bible is a spiritual book, but it is also a history book. Look at history to find out who your people were before they migrated or were taken to whatever land they are in now and were in previously.

If you believe that you are a part of the chosen people that the Bible is centered around, great, but it is okay if you are not of the chosen people. It is a great thing to be a child of Abraham, Isaac, and Jacob but it is an even greater thing to be a child of the Most High God. In the appendix, there is a detailed explanation of who I believe this God and His son are. He is the God of the Hebrews, but He is also the creator of all, so the adherence to the Most High's laws and principles are of the highest benefit to you and anyone who has the mindset of overcoming.

According to the Bible and history, the ancient chosen people were scattered, their temple was destroyed, and all of their knowledge was lost and scattered as well. The New Testament states that this lost and scattered group of people won't come back together in their homeland until the final days, but before that, the Old Testament states there will come a time when these people will lose all knowledge and the inheritance of who they are because of great wickedness and iniquity. This next excerpt is from Jeremiah to the children of Judah.

> *Jeremiah 17:4*
> *4And thou, even thyself, shalt **discontinue from thine heritage** that I gave thee; and I will cause thee to serve thine enemies in the land which thou knowest not: for ye have kindled a fire in mine anger, which shall burn for ever.*

This discontinuance in the form of a dispersion put

everyone on an even playing field. Everyone, even those who believe they are the lost and chosen, has to walk by faith and not by sight. No one can tell who the chosen people are by the eye, so follow the Most High because you believe in Him and not because of who you believe you are. Everyone is now subject to this method of faith. The signs and wonders have greatly slowed for a reason.

SOFT WORDS

There was a time when harsh words were softer. There was less connotation and less bias before the world was programmed using time (continued attention) and frequency (repetition) into what it is now. This was a time when words meant what they were created to mean and people used those words to express what they meant without connotation. These connotations stem from the people who use certain words most frequently in a negative or positive manner. If a word is used by people in a positive light many times over in public and private settings, the word will have a positive connotation. The opposite is also true. Religion is like words because connotations become associated with them, but there was a time when religion also meant what it was created to mean and not what people assume religion means because of the people associated and related to it.

Because of the lack of connotations in times of the past, words were softer. Concepts were multidimensional, but words were flat. When the Bible is read in Hebrew, in many sections and pages, it sounds like it is repeating itself because there weren't many different words to say the same thing, although there were always different parables or examples to illustrate the same concepts. This made the language softer. It was soft like velvet.

THE PERSPECTIVE OF TRUTH

As we go through this journey, this is the question that I want you to ask yourself, "Are the words that I am reading true?" If I told you that flipping a coin has a 50% chance of landing on either heads or tails, but then you actually went to flip the coin ten times and the coin landed on tails seven times, is the 50% probability still true? The answer is yes, it is true. The problem or doubt doesn't lie in the probability. It lies in the fact that you only flipped the coin ten times. In theory, the more that you flip the coin, the closer the outcomes approach the probability, but there are also other variables that can affect the outcome. Is the coin balanced and weighted justly so that it flips evenly? Is the flipping method of the coin unbiased so that it doesn't affect the result? Even though these things can affect the outcome, the probability is true and it is the same for the knowledge in this book.

If you follow the Most High, the probability is extremely high that you will be successful in the short term, but the probability of success is 100% in the long term. The Most High said that if you hearken unto me, I will provide you with what you need and much more. To hearken is not only to listen with your ears but also to listen with your actions. If you follow the Most High but, you are having a hard time and don't perceive yourself to be blessed, is the problem with God and following Him or is the problem with the way you're following? If you flip a coin, there is a 50% chance that what you guess the coin will land on will come true. If the Most High won't forsake you, there is a 100% chance that what He promised will come true and is true.

The probability from the coin example above is the Word. We know that what the scriptures say is true (100%), so we don't have to guess. The coin from the example is the vessel of the outcome. We are the vessels that the Most High uses to fulfill the words in the Bible. The flipping method from the example is your way of following the Most High. Are you following the Most High's words in an unbiased manner that isn't causing your efforts to come to naught? Are your beliefs about God balanced the way He says they should be or have man and the world distorted them?

FISHERS OF MEN

When Christ first started to gather the disciples, he started with four fishermen. He told them to come follow him and that he would make them fishers of men. We, the followers of Christ, are all fishers of men to some extent. He spoke to them from a fishing point of view because that was their expertise and it would be easy to understand what he meant. If they had the capacity to catch fish in nets, then they also had the capacity to use that gift and its concept to catch men in the Most High's salvation. When the miracles were performed when feeding people, what were they eating? Five loaves and two fish. Was it a coincidence that they were eating what four of them specialized in or were the four disciples using their expertise and resources to catch men?

> *James 4:8*
> Let him know, that **he which converteth the sinner from the error** of his way shall save a soul from death, and **shall hide a multitude of sins**.

The goal of this writing is to reveal how to become fishers of men and explain why this is important for your success in the kingdom. Repent for the kingdom is at hand is the slogan of the fisherman. To repent means to turn from your ways and the things that you are doing. To repent for the kingdom means to change what you are doing and follow the ways of the Most High God immediately. If the Kingdom is at hand, the Kingdom is upon us. It's at hand for the fisher and his catch. The fisher and the catch make it to the kingdom by both catching and both being caught. Christ saw men fishing and asked them to come follow him. They immediately put down their nets and left their profession to follow him. Are you willing to put down what is asked of you, whether it be a profession or a vice?

2
THE WAY OF THE FISHERMAN

The way of the fisherman is simple. It's putting the Most High first. This means that if you are going to fear anything in this world, before you fear that, fear God. If you are going to love anything or anyone in this world, love God first. Don't only love God first, also love God more. This prioritizing of the Most High is not for His good but for yours. This action of putting the Most High first is the prime indicator of the priority of your heart.

When you wake up and prayer is the first thing that you do, that is a bright flare to the Most High that He comes before anything else in this world. Yes, you love things like your family greatly, but without Him protecting your family when you're not able to, you will have no family. Know that your ability to protect your family and anything else comes from Him.

Whatever you do, do it first for the Most High. If you can't do it first for the Most High, don't do it all. If you can't hate the Most High, don't hate anyone. Someone would say that it isn't wise to hate the Most High because you would be blocking your blessings and your covering, but when you hate someone else, you block the same blessings and the same covering. Therefore in a sense, when you hate your brother, you hate the Most High. The Most High created you in love, but He did the same for your bother.

THE FISHERMAN'S SAFETY NET

The fisherman's safety net is not designed to catch fish. It's designed to catch the fisherman himself. The fisherman's way is what keeps him safe when he falls or runs into trouble. The four pillars of the fisherman's safety net are thanksgiving/gratitude, the keeping of thy word/vows, calling upon him/prayer, and glorying in the Most High God/giving due credit. Below is an excerpt from Psalms which shows the Most High expressly stating what He wants from his servants. These pillars of how the Most High wants us to please Him are seen multiple times throughout the Bible. Later, we will see how the process is illustrated in the Book of Jonah.

> *Psalm 50:14-15*
> *14 Offer unto God **thanksgiving**; and **pay thy vows** unto the most High:*
> *15 And **call upon me** in the day of trouble: I will deliver thee, and thou shalt **glorify me**.*

3
FOUR PILLARS OF THE FISHERMAN

A pillar is a structure used as support for a building. When Christ started building what we now understand to be the future of faith, he started with four fishermen that were the pillars of his ministry. They were Simon Peter, Andrew, James and John. The Alahayam or Elohim is the foundation, and Christ is the cornerstone of that foundation. This is the rebuilding of the kingdom on Earth as it is in Heaven. The pillars of Christ's teachings are one and the same as those of David. We will now go more in depth with these four pillars found throughout Psalms.

1. THANKSGIVING

Everything starts with an ask. Either you will ask the Most High for something or He will ask you. When you ask, focus on gratitude. Without thanksgiving, there is an inconsistent connection with the Holy Spirit that is asking of you. When there is no spirit of thankfulness within you, what replaces it? If you are not thankful, then what are you? The more thankful you are for any and every thing, the stronger your connection will be with the Spirit.

> Philippians 4:6
> 6Be careful for nothing; but **in every thing by prayer** and supplication **with thanksgiving let your requests be made known unto God**.

Thankfulness for what the Most High is already doing, even the things that are unknown to us, keeps us away from the thin line between prosperity and greed. Thanksgiving makes us not ask for more, but ask for what we can do with what He has already given us. He has given us all the tools to be successful so what we lack is the wisdom to know how and when to use the tools. This is where following the voice of the Spirit comes in.

If you have a hammer in your hand, should the front flat part be used to build or should the fork at the rear of the hammer be used to demolish? Should the flat front portion of the hammer be used to demolish or should the fork portion of the hammer be used to pull a nail hammered at the wrong angle? Pulling the nail gives an opportunity for the nail to be reset properly; a second chance. All of these options create different outcomes. The answers to these questions are what the voice of the Spirit gives us.

Without this voice, we may make the right choice at the wrong time or the wrong choice at the right time. How do you know the difference? Discernment. When you're building, should you be correcting by pulling out nails laid in error or should you be adding more nails to strengthen the nails that are slightly crooked? Should you pull nails and lay new ones or lay the same nail in a different position? Discernment. Discernment comes through asking.

Thankfulness keeps you present and culls your avarice. Desire for more is only needed for a specific purpose in completing a mission for the Most High. Having a desire for more without a purpose is greed. Greed has no intentions for the "more" that it desires. It wants more just for the sake of having more. If you aren't thankful now with everything that He has done and the opportunities that He has provided, when will you ever be thankful? Remember that desire and greed are your flesh's nature, but thanksgiving is the nature of the spirit.

Thankfulness must come now because you don't know how your success is going to look. You could be one day away from what you consider success, so if you are moving with the Most High, you have to assume with hope that He is taking you in the right direction. If this is the case, be thankful now and forever more.

There is a chemical reaction in your brain when you receive a compliment or someone does something nice for you. You then respond with thank you. The things that the Most High does for you are like compliments or being given nice things. Your perspective of the world changes how your brain processes chemicals, so when you recognize what the Most High has done and say thank you, no matter how great or how small the deed, there is also a chemical reaction. Continuously be grateful, and your mood is sure to change. Try it and see.

> Instruction: Every time a thought about gratitude or being thankful comes to mind, thank the Most High verbally. Also, internally (non-verbally) thank the Most High with all of your being. Make it a habit to thank the Most High for the good things and the bad things, because His ways are not our ways. Many times, bless-

ings come in disguise for those who remain faithful. Remain faithful by remaining thankful; specifically thankful to the Most High. Give thanks as if what you need to be done is already done because it is.

---

2. VOWS OF THE LIPS

When you say that you're going to do something, do it. We were made in the Most High's image so along with our physical makeup, we should also reflect His principles and characteristics. The hallmark characteristic of the Most High is that His Word is true. If His words were not true, He could not say let there be light, and have light exist. It exists now because the words were true.

> *Psalm 160:160*
> *160* Thy word is true from *the beginning: and every one of thy righteous judgments* endureth *for ever.*

It is of utmost importance to keep the covenant that you confess with your mouth and to keep true to the words that you say to the Most High and to other men. Why is it also to other men? Because on this road as a fisher of men, you will be a representative/servant of the Most High. If you claim to represent the Most High and that He sent you, but don't keep your word, people may think that that's indicative of the Most High. The Most High is always true to His Word and keeps His Word.

The relationship between a parent and a child is reciprocal. The Most High works like a parent and earthly parents require obedience of their children in exchange for the resources bestowed upon them. The Father requires you to live a certain way in exchange for the covering and blessings that He promised you. It's called a covenant or a testament. This is the covenant between Jacob and the Most High.

God's Spoken Vow to Jacob:

Genesis 28:13-15
13 *And, behold, the LORD stood above it, and said, I am the LORD God of Abraham thy father, and the God of Isaac: the land whereon thou liest, to thee will I give it, and to thy seed;*
14 *And thy seed shall be as the dust of the earth, and thou shalt spread abroad to the west, and to the east, and to the north, and to the south: and in thee and in thy seed shall all the families of the earth be blessed.*
15 *And, behold, I am with thee, and will keep thee in all places whither thou goest, and will bring thee again into this land; for I will not leave thee, until I have done that which I have spoken to thee of.*

Jacobs Spoken Vow to God

Genesis 28:20-22
20 *And Jacob vowed a vow, saying, If God will be with me, and will keep me in this way that I go, and will give me bread to eat, and raiment to put on,*

> *21 So that I come again to my father's house in peace; then shall the LORD be my God:*
> *22 And this stone, which I have set for a pillar, shall be God's house: and of all that thou shalt give me I will surely give the tenth unto thee.*

What will you do for the Most High? When you pray is it all one sided or do you tell Him what you desire to do for Him as well? Don't wait for your situation to be perfect before vowing. Is your life perfect? Will everything ever be exactly the way that you want it? The Bible didn't say that the Most High will be perfect to you by giving you the perfect life. What it does say is that He will be just, fair, and merciful.

Instruction: The next time you pray, don't only request things from the Most High but also tell Him what you intend to do or sacrifice in return for what you ask for. Tell the Father your plan. Verbalize it. This too must be done with the gratitude from the first pillar.

---

3. MAKING THE CALL

The Most High wants you to call upon Him in the day of trouble. This call upon Him means to speak with your tongue. Yes, the Most High knows what is in your heart, but the heart only confirms that you truly mean what you say when you vow or make the call. Many times, when you call upon the Most High, you will tell Him that you will never do whatever act you just committed again or you may be praying for the ability to overcome the consequences of such acts. These words are the call that you are making to the Most High, but they also may contain in them the vows of your lips. In the times of your calamity, the Most High wants to be the one that you lean upon. In Proverbs 3:5, it says to trust in the Lord with all your heart. When you're in trouble, you want to depend on someone or something that you can trust.

> *Psalm 18:2-3*
> 2 *The LORD is my rock, and my fortress, and my deliverer; my God, my strength,* **in whom I will trust***; my buckler, and the horn of my salvation,* and *my high tower.*
> 3 **I will call upon the LORD**, who is worthy *to be praised:* **so shall I be saved** *from mine enemies.*

"Trouble" doesn't have to be the type of trouble that includes danger or an emergency. It can also be the type of trouble you encounter when you have a problem in your life regarding things like business, relationships, or agriculture. If you don't have the answer or the proper knowledge to complete your task, He is the answer. That's when you need to call upon Him. This is the time that you're likely to receive the instructions regarding these problems. Call on Him in your prayers. The reason you need to be delivered is because you most likely initially misheard the instructions after prayer, went astray from the instructions or didn't receive the full instructions yet. This is okay. The Father's voice is here to guide you.

After you make the call unto the Most High, listen. Your ability to hear the Spirit comes not only by practice but by trust and experience. He will without a doubt deliver you if that is what is best for you. We have to have trust in the wisdom of the Most High because we are in the positions that we are in for a reason. Observe carefully to see if you can figure out why you're in that position.

> *John 16:13-14*
> 13*Howbeit when he, the* **Spirit of truth**, *is come, he* **will guide you into all truth**: *for he shall not speak of himself; but whatsoever he shall hear, that shall he speak: and he will shew you things to come.*
> 14*He shall glorify me: for* **he shall receive of mine, and shall shew** *it* **unto you.**

Instruction: Make it a habit to consider the Most High in everything that you do. Call upon His wisdom whenever making a decision or thinking through a choice, issue, or obstacle.

---

4. GLORIFICATION

> *John 17:4*
> 4***I have glorified thee on the earth***: *I have finished* ***the work which thou gavest me*** *to do.*

Your deliverance from trouble is proclaimed. This means that if you are a child of the Most High and you call upon Him in your day of trouble with all your heart, He will surely deliver you according to His plan. When you are delivered, you must remember to give the Most High the proper glory and praise. Don't give anything else credit above the Most High. If you do, you are signifying to others that those things delivered you and not the Most High. If you give yourself credit, you are making yourself an idol by saying that you delivered yourself. Every step is important and should be remembered for your success. This is the way.

Glorification of the Most High and thanksgiving are tightly intertwined. In fact, glorifying the Most High is just giving thanksgiving verbally and openly for the things that you have accomplished or the outcomes that you have attained. The end of the process is the beginning of the process of the four pillars; thus creating a never ending cycle of exaltation.

> *Psalm 75:9*
> *9But **I will declare for ever**; I will sing praises to the God of Jacob.*

Instruction: In thanksgiving, you receive instruction. Adhere to that instruction. When trouble arises, you call upon your instructor (the Father). Your instructor delivers you and then you give your instructor credit in your exalted position. Now, the instructor will be glorified and exalted. This is the way.

> *Psalm 66:13-17*
> *13I will go into thy house with burnt offerings: I will **pay thee my vows**,*
> *14Which **my lips have uttered**, and my **mouth hath spoken**, when I was **in trouble**.*
> *15I will offer unto thee burnt sacrifices of fatlings, with the incense of rams; I will offer bullocks with goats. **Selah**.*
> *16Come and **hear**, all ye that **fear God**, and I will declare what **He hath done** for my soul.*

*17I **cried** unto him **with my mouth**, and he was **extolled with my tongue**.*

Extol
- to praise highly: glorify

4
THE FISHERMAN'S TALE OF JONAH

Jonah is one of the greatest examples in the Bible of someone being asked to be a fisherman. Why? Because the entire book of Jonah is based on a simple request from the Most High for Jonah to pull out a fishing pole and fish for men. The book of Jonah is a warning and an encouragement to all that are called. Let's take a look at what lessons we can learn.

> *Jonah 1:1-3a*
> *1Now* **the word of the LORD came unto Jonah** *the son of Amittai,* **saying***,*
> *2Arise,* **go to Nineveh***, that great city, and* **cry against it***; for their wickedness is come up before me.*
> *3****But Jonah rose up to flee*** *unto Tarshish* ***from the presence of the LORD****,*

The initial request from the Word of the Most High was for Jonah to go and speak to the people of Nineveh. The Most High asked Jonah to go rebuke Nineveh because he was capable of completing the task. Instead of being obedient, Jonah went elsewhere. His disobedience caused the Most High to send chastisement in the form of two inescapable trials.

The first trial was a great tempest, which was a wind storm on the sea. The magnitude of this storm was high enough to convince others to cry out and submit to the Most High God. The second trial was the Most High preparing a whale to swallow Jonah. In Jonah 1 and 2 (below), there are two depictions of this process where calamity comes, thanksgiving (fear) is given, sacrifices and vows are made, deliverance occurs, and credit for salvation is given.

Men on the Boat Using the Pillars

Jonah 1:14-16
14 Wherefore they **cried unto the LORD, and said, We beseech thee, O LORD**, *we beseech thee, let us not perish for this man's life, and lay not upon us innocent blood: for thou,* **O LORD, hast done as it pleased thee.**
15 *So they* **took up Jonah, and cast him forth** *into the sea: and the sea ceased from her raging.*
16 **Then the men feared the LORD exceedingly**, *and* **offered a sacrifice** *unto the LORD, and* **made vows.**

Jonah Using the Pillars

> *Jonah 2:7-10*
> 7 When my soul fainted within me I remembered the LORD: and **my prayer came in unto thee**, into thine holy temple.
> 8 They that **observe lying vanities** forsake their own mercy.
> 9 But **I will sacrifice unto thee with the voice of thanksgiving**; I will **pay that that I have vowed. Salvation is of the LORD.**
> 10 And the LORD spake unto the fish, and it vomited out Jonah upon the dry land.

IMMEDIATELY AFTER SUBMISSION to the Most High deliverance from the trials occurred. Are you going through a trial right now? Are you in a proverbial storm or belly of a fish? What can you do about it?

Religion likes to tell us how the Most High works, but if we observe the patterns of the Most High ourselves, we wouldn't need anyone to tell us how He works. We are able to test and prove it for ourselves. Try the way of the fisherman for a month to see if it is real. If it works for a month, it will and can work for a year. If it works for a year, it can and will work for a lifetime. The rest of this book goes into the details and components of the methods, the walk, the trials and the way of the fisherman. Continue reading if you are willing to try the way.

5

DOMINION OVER ALL

Domination over the inner man is the 1st task of power.

What is strength? In order to follow the Most High and His instructions, you need a domineering will. This will far exceeds the will of Michael Jordan to win his first 3peat and even his second. The amount of will needed to overcome your flesh and obey the Spirit is so great that the will of the entire world pales in comparison. This will is so great that it makes the waves of the sea look like ripples in a puddle. That's why someone with true strength can speak to the sea and it listens. It's because talking to your flesh is harder to do than talking to water, even if it's the sea.

We can look at addicts to get an idea of how strong the flesh is. I've seen addicts do things for drugs that they wouldn't do for God. I've seen addicts betray their family with tears in their eyes to get their next fix. How strong was the hold on that person's mind and body?

Overcoming addiction, vices, and habits is equal to overcoming the world. Whatever you can/have overcome, you are greater than. The term overcome means to become higher or to surmount. You literally have to be higher in mind and spirit than your flesh.

The Most High gave our fleshly bodies, even in sin, dominion over this world so that if we master dominion over our flesh, we conquer the world. We conquer the world not only in flesh but also in the spirit. We must overcome the flesh to not do wrong but equally and to the same degree, to do right. This dominion is the same as having the ability to love at all times and with an unshakable love. Being able to love relentlessly is equal to overcoming hate or some other negative emotion such as jealousy.

> *Romans 8:37-39*
> *37Nay,* ***in all these things we are more than conquerors through him that loved us.***
> *38For I am persuaded, that* ***neither death, nor life, nor angels, nor principalities, nor powers, nor things present, nor things to come,***
> *39**Nor height, nor depth, nor any other creature, shall be able to separate us from the love of God**, which is in Christ our Lord.*

You will not reach the pinnacle during your journey without completing this step. This is not to say that you won't complete your journey by attempting to accomplish this step over and over. Unwavering courage and faith to keep moving forward during this step can work wonders. Every fisherman on the straight and narrow must be led by his heart. He is led by his heart because of the new commandment Christ spoke of that is also written in Jeremiah 31.

> *Jeremiah 31:32-33*
>
> *32***Not according to the covenant that I made with their fathers** *in the day* that *I took them by the hand to bring them out of the land of Egypt; which my covenant they brake, although I was an husband unto them, saith the LORD:*
>
> *33But* **this shall be the covenant that I will make with the house of Israel;** *After those days, saith the LORD,* **I will put my law in their inward parts, and write it in their hearts;** *and will be their God, and they shall be my people.*

After attaining dominion over one's self fully, while living with a pure heart attained by following the laws written on it, you will have now acquired power. You have to make it a point to remember to use it. The stronger you become through the domination of listening to the Spirit, the more power you'll have. This power is only to do the duty of a fisherman fully. It is not for personal gain. You won't need to gain anything personally because your needs will already be taken care of.

THE POWER OF DOMINATION

If you were going to tell a shark what to do, you would be trying to get the shark to overcome his natural programming and obey a command you received and gave the shark in the spirit. In comparison to the thought processes and attacks from evil that a human undergoes, the shark's natural programming and fleshly nature is simple. The shark never has to doubt his instinct or nature to swim, eat, and reproduce, but we, as man, doubt how we do the equivalent to these. In fact, most sharks are following the law written on their hearts or the law given to them by mother nature, the Holy Spirit, flawlessly. They are relentlessly following what is written in their flesh. The difference is that the law written in what would be their spirits/souls and the law written in their flesh are one and the same. In man, the laws of the flesh and the spirit are totally different.

God made man a little lower than an angel, so we have the flesh of the animal and the spirit like an angel. Animal's assignment is to obey their flesh. In the Bible, the animals didn't disobey the Most High, and it was easy for them to accomplish. In contrast, the angel's assignment was to obey their spirit's nature, because they had no flesh. The task of the Spirit is to obey a higher type of order from the Most High. In this task, choice is given because following the Most High has to be a choice made willingly. Someone being forced to follow the Most High may not be following the Most High at all. They may just be trying to survive.

We can see that some angels clearly disobeyed the Most High in the Bible and were cast out of Heaven. They were sent to earth with the flesh followers, animals, that aren't bound to obeying the law of the spirit. Man has both, the battle of flesh and the battle of Spirit combined into one. This is why man has dominion over animals and spirits. If man can defeat the fleshly and spiritual attacks, he will be stronger than both. This is partially shown by Christ.

Christ already dominated the Spirit world/the world of creation and was/is the master of it, but it was upon him to also be sent here to overcome the world of the flesh in the flesh. That's why we are brothers with Christ. Man and Christ both had/have to overcome the flesh and evil spirits so we are on the same journey; the journey of an obedient spirit that was put on earth to overcome the flesh and become a rewarded spirit once again. This is what it means when it says that the Most High knew you before the womb. He knew if we had an obedient spirit or not, and even knowing this, it is also said that we were born in sin

Did you have an obedient spirit like the Great I AM or a rebellious spirit like Lucifer? The answer to this question is also why it is upon the fishermen, those chosen before birth with dominion over their flesh, to obtain/retain dominion over their own spirits so that they can convert our brother's with disobedient spirits. When you convert a soul, you are literally dominating the adversary spiritually by dominating your flesh. This is harder and greater than dominating flesh, animals and elements (water). Retaining dominion over your own spirit is how you receive power through the Most High. You have to take dominion righteously to receive power. Someone can make you ruler, but no one can force you to lead. You were highly made with all capability to overcome and rule.

> *1 John 5:3-4*
> *3For **this is the love of God**, that we **keep his commandments**: and his commandments are not grievous.*
> *4For whatsoever is **born of God overcometh** the world: and **this is the victory that overcometh the world**, even **our faith**.*

Even in dominion, you will still face storms. Storms are a form of trial or tribulation. Everyone will face storms, but with dominion, storms will work in your favor. The winds of the storm will blow seeds onto your land rather than uprooting valuable crops and trees.

Regardless of how bad the storm seems, when you're in obedience the storm is working to your benefit, and when you're in disobedience the storm is working to correct your ways so that one day, you can receive a benefit. An example is the storm that Jonah faced before being thrown off the boat. Jonah was sleeping in the boat during the storm and had no way to stop the storm due to his disobedience. The only way to relieve the other mariners of the storm was to throw Jonah off the boat. When we compare and contrast that with Christ, there is a lot to be learned. The difference between a willing fisherman with dominion and an unwilling fisherman in disobedience is vast. A tempest arose in the same way for Christ as it did for Jonah, so let us take a look at how Christ handled it differently.

> *Mark 4:37–39*
> 37 And there arose **a great storm of wind**, and the waves **beat into the ship**, so that it was now full.
> 38 And he was in the hinder part of the ship, asleep on a pillow: and they awake him, and say unto him, Master, carest thou not that we perish?
> 39 And **he arose, and rebuked the wind, and said unto** the sea, **Peace, be still**. And the wind ceased, and **there was a great calm**.

Christ was able to wake up and speak to the tempest in the storming sea with his faith and dominion. Jonah was not capable of this at the time because of his disobedience. This dominion is the result of Christ's unwavering obedience and love.

> *Proverbs 18:21*
> 21 Death and life are in the power of the tongue: and they that love it shall eat the fruit thereof.

Once the Spirit (voice) talks to you, it is upon you to talk to the world. This Voice will be discussed in great detail in the next chapter. The things that you speak into this world with your tongue are what you will reap. Part of the reason for this is because words are images. You can only talk about something for so long before you start to mentally imagine it. You can't talk about red velvet cake for an hour without picturing what it looks like. Does it have frosting? How vivid is the red? Then your mind will start to wonder or has already made up how sweet the cake is.

Speaking is the beginning of creation. The Most High spoke the world into existence. Let there be light. He spoke with His Voice, then He saw (eye) the image/light (Christ) of what He spoke.

> *Genesis 1:3-4*
> *3 And God **said**, Let there be light: and there was light.*
> *4 And God **saw** the light, that it was good: and God divided the light from the darkness.*

While unflinchingly following the commandments written on your heart, when you speak, things will come to pass. You will start to not only feel empowered, but be empowered. When you loose something, things are loosed. When you bind something, things are bound. This is the dominion given to every child of the Most High. Speak and it will be spoken to. This is why we must be exact in what we order while praying. Don't assume anything about the Most High except His goodness.

Instruction: Purity of the pinnacle is absolute. You can't halfway remove sin and achieve full power. Remove it completely to the best of your ability for as long as you can. Then do it again. If you're noticing that the world isn't responding to your dominion, there may be something that you are partaking in that you need to strip away. Consider everything. Obey the Most High and the world will obey you.

6
THE VOICE OF DOMINATION

Galatians 4:6
*6And **because ye are sons, God hath sent forth the Spirit of his Son into your hearts, crying**, Abba, Father.*

In John 14, Christ, the greatest fisherman, says that he had to leave the disciples for two very important reasons. First, he left to prepare a place for us and second, to become an intercessor on our behalf. His intercession is to plead our prayers and requests to the Most High. He also said that he would not leave us alone while he was gone, so the promise of companionship was given. It's important to remember, the companion that we have in his absence does come with a stipulation of obedience.

John 14:15-16
*15**If ye love me, keep my commandments.***
*16And I will pray the Father, **and he shall give you another Comforter**, that he may abide with you for ever;*

The stipulation is that you keep Christ's commandments. His commandments are HEAR, O Israel; The Lord our God is one Lord; to love the Lord thy God with all thy heart, and with all thy soul, and with all thy mind and after this, the next is to love thy neighbor as thyself. We keep his commandments and in return, we receive open access or an ear to hear the companion. We must truly understand what this means because following this is our evidence of love.

> *John 14:17*
> 17Even **the Spirit of truth**; *whom* **the world cannot receive, because it seeth him not, neither knoweth him**: *but ye* **know him**; *for he dwelleth with you, and* **shall be in you**.

Once the love of Christ is established, you will have uninhibited companionship with the Comforter. The Comforter is the Holy Spirit/Spirit of Truth. Without love, you cannot hear the instructions of the Spirit. Notice, that I am not saying that the Spirit is not speaking to you; it is just that you may be ignoring it or not able to properly comprehend it. Without love, your connection to the Spirit will be weak. Without love, you are of the world so you can't see, know, or receive the Spirit, but those who follow the commandments of Christ know this voice because the Spirit lives in you and dwells in your heart.

> *John 14:25-26*
> 25These **things have I spoken unto you**, *being yet present with you.*
> 26**But the Comforter, which is the Holy Ghost**, *whom the Father will send in my name,* **he shall teach you all things, and bring**

all things to your remembrance, *whatsoever I have said unto you.*

The Comforter wasn't sent in vain. It was sent to teach us what we need to know about all the things that we have forgotten. Previously, we forgot the purpose and use of knowledge, how to hear instruction, and how the voice of the Spirit sounds. This isn't just aimless knowledge that is being given by the Comforter. This is the knowledge that will guide us on this road to further building the Kingdom by fishing for men. This instruction is a continuation of the things that Christ spoke.

Christ spoke words not of himself but of the Father that sent him. If ever you need to know something, ask first of the Most High and you will be shown where and how to attain the knowledge. When you ask of the Most High, He responds through the Comforter. Thus, the instructions Christ gave and the instructions from the Comforter are one and the same. The Comforter/Spirit comes in the form of an internal voice. Christ followed directions from the Holy Spirit as well. Here, you will see Christ being led of the Spirit up to the mount. If Christ was led of the Spirit, every fisherman should be.

Matthew 4
*1 **Then was the Son of God led up of the Spirit** into the wilderness to be tempted of the devil.*
2 And when he had fasted forty days and forty nights, he was afterward an hungred.

Time for thought: Take a moment to review your ways. Are you receiving warnings and suggestions from the Spirit but ignoring them? Where does the Comforter fit in with your daily life? Do you have a conscious relationship with the Comforter? Are you even aware of the presence of the Comforter? Can you identify the Comforter actively working in your life?

In the Bible, the Comforter is sometimes referred to as a he and sometimes as a she. Don't let this perturb or distract you. The Comforter is a spirit. The Holy Spirit is the evidence of the new covenant.

> *Hebrews 10:15-16*
> *15 Whereof* **the Holy Ghost also is a witness to us***: for after* **that he had said before,**
> *16* **This is the covenant** *that I will make with them after those days, saith the Lord,* **I will put my laws into their hearts, and in their minds** *will* **I write them***;*

The above verse expressly states that the Holy Spirit is a witness to us. Witnesses observe, record, and talk. They tell you what they know, have seen, or have heard. The Holy Spirit is the witness (Voice) that speaks into our hearts and our minds the commands and the Word that we should follow. Reread this verse above. It is clearly stated. The Holy Spirit is one of the three that bear record.

DAVID ON THE FRONTIER OF FAITH

David is the first in the Bible to proclaim this method of instruction for salvation. He stated that continual sacrifices were no longer acceptable unto the Most High if the heart was not pure. This is in stark contrast to Saul, the king prior to David, who attempted to offer a sacrifice instead of following a direct order from the Most High regarding

Amalek. David was following the way of Christ before Christ manifested in the flesh.

> *Psalm 40:6-8*
> *6**Sacrifice and offering thou didst not desire; mine ears hast thou opened**: burnt offering and sin offering hast thou not required.*
> *7Then said I, Lo, I come: in the volume of the book it is written of me,*
> *8I delight to do thy will, O my God: yea, **thy law is within my heart.***

David foretells of a time where the law of sacrifices and circumcision would not be enough. If we are to be justified by the law, we have to follow the entirety of the law, but because of the wickedness in our hearts, that law became of no effect. Israel was sacrificing and following the law, but there was no love in their hearts. Without love in the heart how can one receive of the Comforter?

> *1 Peter 1:22-23*
> *22Seeing ye have **purified** your souls in **obeying the truth through the Spirit unto unfeigned love of the brethren**, see that ye **love one another with a pure heart** fervently:*
> *23Being **born again**, not of corruptible seed, but of incorruptible, **by the word of God**, which liveth and abideth for ever.*

The word "domination" is used because if you don't approach this voice with the right perspective and attitude, you will succumb to the adversary. The will that a fisher performs is of the Most High, but the willpower must come from you. The power to do anything comes from the Father, but the power of choice is yours. This is the strongest and only true power that you have. Your power to decide should be in the front of your mind at all times. Willpower is based on your power of choice.

We are really weaklings that have been told that we are powerful. We have been separated from our true and original power. Now, the most powerful thing that you can choose or decide to do is to love; not just any manmade love but love according to knowledge. Don't love according to zeal. Love according to knowledge. This knowledge is of the Word written in the book and also of the Word written in your heart, ye with a pure heart.

Instruction: Listen for the voice of truth and righteousness in all decisions and activities that you are involved in. If you are following the four pillars, you will definitely be able to hear the Voice. Find the love of the brethren by finding love for the brethren within. Start treating your brethren how you treat yourself, literally. This also means to treat yourself how you treat your brother. Start within your immediate family and then branch out.

7
CONTROLLING THE LIGHT

Matthew 6:22
22 The **light of the body is the eye**: if therefore thine **eye be single**, thy **whole body** shall be **full of light**.

You need a fully functioning light to see where you are going on this road. The light of the body is the eye. The eye of the body is the mind. The mind has the capability to be full of light or full of darkness.

When you focus your mind's eye on a single righteous goal, your thoughts will follow. For example, if the righteous thought that you are holding in focus is a book, your thoughts will become the process. While focusing, you must be keenly aware of the thoughts that are coming to you. There will be an idea among many that is the way. An idea of a page will be contained in those thoughts; and on that page you will write one single sentence at a time by writing one single word at a time by writing one single letter at a time by writing one single stroke at a time.

THE POWER OF THE MIND'S EYE

When I say pink pony, you see in your mind a pink pony. You are not using your two physical eyes to see this pink pony, but you can still see it. The tool that you are using to see this pink pony is your mind's eye. This is the eye of the body that the Bible refers to in Matthew 6.

The mind's eye is the cornerstone of how we use faith and hope on our journey of purpose. When we pray and have faith for somebody to be healed from a broken leg, we see an image in our mind of the person walking, using the leg, or the leg being healed. When you pray for someone to come out of a coma, you don't envision them sleeping; you envision them woke or waking up, and operating at their usual capacity. Envisioning the desired outcome in our mind is a part of faith, hope, prayer, and belief.

Be mindful enough to control your mind's eye. Whatever you focus on is being put into motion through faith just by thinking on it. This is why we must guard against negative thoughts. A negative mind can lead us to negative places because holding a negative thought in your mind is equivalent to believing it will/can come true.

Why would a negative thought be active in your mind if you didn't believe it was possible? This is the same for positive thoughts. Why would you hold a positive thought in your mind if you didn't believe it could come true. We only holdfast to the thoughts, whether negative or positive, that we believe can come true. When is the last time you held onto the thought of flying through the air like Superman? You haven't.

LEAD WITH YOUR MIND'S EYE

Leading with your mind's eye means to lead with faith. While the long-term destination is the Kingdom, the short-term destination is your goal/focus based around the gift that you are currently utilizing. This waypoint on your journey is where you believe the Most High is taking you through your gifts and abilities. If your light is focused on your waypoint, don't be concerned with whether or not you're traveling the wrong way. Decide the path and commit, as long as the Spirit commands and allows. Many times we focus on the direction of the path more than walking. Taking the next step is always the next step.

> *Psalm 32:8*
> *8**I will instruct thee and teach thee in the way** which thou shalt go: **I will guide thee with mine eye.***

THE LOWER LIGHT

There is a second light in the body. If the main light of the body is the eye, then it is like the sun, and the second lesser/lower light in the body is like the moon in that it reflects the light of the eye in the same way that the moon reflects the light of the sun. This light is located in the bowels and in the lower organs. For example, when you watch something arousing using the main light that is the eye, it is reflected in the lower eye, which is the reproductive organs, by hardness of the penis or wetness of the vagina.

When you watch something like a commercial that contains food that is visually flavorful or appealing to the eye, which is the light of the mind, it is reflected in your bowels (stomach). Your stomach may start to grumble, and you will, almost like magic, develop a hunger or desire for the pizza, burger, french fries, or soda which you saw in the commercial advertisement. The eye (light) of the mind controls the minor eye (lesser light). This is why companies like Apple, McDonalds, and Alphabet (Google) spend billions on advertising. It's because advertising works. They know that your eyes are vulnerable. If they can get an image to your eye (sun), they can reflect the desired response in your body (moon).

The lesser light is also called a "light" because it is where the spark is derived and/or contained that gives life. These bowels (members) can give actual life, but if used wrongly, they can also become infected and bring death through situation and disease.

> *Romans 7:21-23*
> *21I find then a law, that, when I would do good, evil is present with me.*
> *22For I delight in the law of God after the inward man:*
> *23But I see another **law in my members**, warring against the **law of my mind**, and bringing me into captivity to the law of sin which is in my members.*

To fight these diseases, one must have either knowledge or trust in the unknown. If you have knowledge, you understand herbs, plants and roots. You can wield nature through the consumption of plants and their derivatives to fix yourself and others. This knowledge, wisdom and understanding are a gift of the Most High and His Voice. Be ye not fooled.

If you have trust in the unknown, you trust in a science that you may or may not understand and you also have to trust intermediaries, companies, and governance that claim to want to make sure that you receive the right medicine. If you didn't receive the right medicine, there is surely more medicine available to battle your original illness, and the illness brought upon by medicinal side effects.

Now that we know this, it is up to us to guard our light. Why? Because it's susceptible and vulnerable beyond our control. Once an image hits our eye we are involuntarily influenced. We still have a choice in what we will do but the body can't stop itself from getting aroused while watching an adult movie and it can't stop itself from getting hungry or its mouth watering when seeing/smelling food. The best that we can do is to remove ourselves from an atmosphere or close our lights. Matthew 6 speaks about our eye either being full of light or darkness. There is no in between.

> *Matthew 6:23*
> *23But if thine eye be evil, thy whole body shall be full of darkness.* ***If therefore the light that is in thee be darkness, how great is that darkness!***

KEEP THE LIGHT ON

When your body is full of darkness, you must feed the lights of the body (the sun and the moons) with light. Your entire being needs light; Spiritually (Word/Roll), Mentally (faith/meditation), and Physically (vegetation/medicine). If you are focused on these three things, thine eye will be single.

> *Ezekiel 3:1-4*
> *1Moreover he said unto me,* ***Son of man, eat that thou findest; eat this roll****, and* ***go speak***
> *unto the house of Israel.*
> *2So I opened my mouth, and he caused me to eat that roll.*

> *3.And he said unto me, Son of man, cause thy belly to eat, and **fill thy BOWELS with this roll** that I give thee. Then did I eat it; and it was in my mouth as honey for sweetness.*
> *4.And he said unto me, **Son of man**, go, get thee unto the house of Israel, and **speak with my words** unto them.*

This excerpt from Ezekiel 3 is about how to control your bowels or your members. You control them with the scroll/roll, which is the Word that is Christ. The reason why you need control over them is so that you can act as Christ did and speak as a fisherman.

MULTIPLE MOONS

There is a second moon as well. This is called the ear, but it will not be discussed in detail now. The ear is similar to the first moon, but instead of being reflected onto from the sun (eye), the ear (2nd moon) reflects to the sun and that light bounces to the first moon, which is the lower organs. This moon also participates in the influence of the lower organs, the same way a jingle keeps the thought of food in your mind. McDonald's jingle is "badop bop bah bah... I'm loving it." You may already be picturing french fries or a Big Mac in your mind. Even the thought of the sound can trigger a mental image in your internal eye that is then reflected in your stomach as hunger.

The reason why the second moon (the ear) has its own light source is because it is where we hear the Word, praises of God, and potentially, from the Most High. The uniqueness of the ear is that you can't close them. If a sound is loud enough, you will still hear it. When your ears are completely protected, there is still an internal dialogue that you can hear that never stops.

PERCEIVING DARKNESS

Darkness comes from chasing something in the past that can't be attained because light is current. You can't go back to the past because there is no light there. Darkness also comes by over pursuing something in the future that hasn't been revealed by light. Now, we see through a glass darkly because the reveal is not complete.

Splitting your persistent thought with the past, present, and future is equivalent to splitting your eye (mind). Most of the time when you're splitting your thought consistently, it is for things that are already taken care of or promised to you. These things are food, shelter, raiment, and companionship (promise of the seed). If these things are already promised, there is no need to split. Splitting, in this instance, signifies worry, doubt, and disbelief.

The goal of things like advertising is to split your thoughts. Advertisers want your mental real estate spread out. If they can attain access to your attention (mind) consistently, it all but guarantees that you will be a customer. Ads place artificial desires towards things that you don't really need. Therefore, give them no thought and also take no thought for the things promised.

> *Philippians 3:13-15*
> *13Brethren, I count not myself to have apprehended:*
> *but* **this one thing** *I do, forgetting those things which are behind, and reaching forth unto those things which are before,*
> *14I press toward the mark for the prize of the high calling of God in Christ.*

> *15 Let us therefore, as many as be perfect,* **be thus minded***: and if in any thing ye be otherwise minded,* **God shall reveal even this unto you***.*

Light reveals all. If you are trying to force something to happen or attain something that is meant for you in the future by doing something of darkness now, you will never receive it how you expect. Shortly after you do receive it, something is destined to go wrong, especially if you are one of the Father's children. This is when you can expect chastisement. All good things come by righteousness and light. An example of this is when you have prayed for something over and over, but it hasn't happened or come; a man may then resort to robbing or a woman may resort to selling her body. They saw themselves with something that they desired in their mind's eye and they dwelt on something so long that they took the matter into their owns hands. No. Leave it in God's hands.

> Instruction: Before actively using the eye, observe it passively. Look and see what your eye is preoccupied with. This will shine a light on where and how you need to direct your light. There are six total lights in the body that make up the eye. See if you can perceive them. Once you understand your eye and its preoccupancy, direct it by focusing on that thought that is the way. This is the beginning of your path.

8
PRESENTED AS A SERVANT

When approaching someone, always prioritize the intention of saving or preserving a person's soul before your personal desires or business dealings with them. If whatever intention you have of interacting with someone can't be accomplished without harm or the person perceiving themselves as being harmed, it is better not to interact. You can still interact with people normally without forcing your beliefs on others, but when the opportunity does present itself to introduce salvation to a person, your past interactions greatly influence the situation. You don't want someone to reject the love of Christ because they are rejecting you or something that you have done. Walk as a servant before you walk as a prince. This is the difference between helping someone and commanding someone to get help.

1 Thessalonians 5:22
22 Abstain from all appearance of evil.

THE DECEPTION OF WHAT'S SEEN

Just as important as not doing anything evil, is looking like you're not doing any evil thing. This is due to a couple of reasons. First, you may bring unwanted persecution and judgement upon yourself because the visual evidence or opticals make you look guilty. People can only judge based upon what they can observe. Your intention or sometimes even the truth cannot be seen. This is why Christ said judge not lest ye be judged.

> *Matthew 7:1-2*
> *1* **Judge not**, *that ye be not judged.* 2 **For with what judgment ye judge, ye shall be judged**: *and with what measure ye mete, it shall be measured to you again.*

You have to understand that regardless of the evidence or what you think you know, there are going to be times when you may be wrong. Your earthly vision, perception, and judgement are imperfect. A good judge knows that only the Most High knows the truth. As you age, this will become more and more clear. Even if something is seen on video or in person, something as simple as the angle can change your perception. I can't tell you how many times a basketball foul looked like a flagrant foul until I saw the other angle in a replay and sometimes the player that I thought was fouled didn't even get touched at all. This is why grace and mercy should be your first reaction to most situations.

The second reason is that, for you to appear to be doing evil, somebody has to see you. It's an appearance. If someone that you have influence over perceives that you are doing evil, but you are not, they may follow the misperception of you doing evil to do evil themselves because of your influence.

That's not your intention, but it can still happen. Our job and duty is to lead people to the Kingdom and not to do evil.

The appearance of evil doesn't always include you being the actual appearance. It also means that you have to refrain from allowing evil to appear in front of you. You don't want to look evil to others, but at the same time, you also don't want to be involved in or absorb the appearance of evil; even evil as an image. As discussed earlier, the appearances of images have an involuntary effect over you. When children grow up with violence in the home, they are affected even though it may not be apparent at the time of the affection. For example, if a child grows up in a home where a man is putting his hands on a woman, as a male, he is more likely to put his hands on a woman. If the child is a female, she's more likely to allow hands to be put upon her or to put her hands on someone else. This influence is involuntary. What you receive in your eyes as an image affects you involuntarily.

LAW OF NATURE

The first law of nature is imitation or in other words, monkey see monkey do. Our mind must be filled with images of the Most High. That includes the words (images) of the Bible and the short-term images of what you believe the Most High has you destined to do.

The nature to imitate is seen early in children. Children can see and have sight well before they can talk. Even though they can hear, they can't understand what you're saying. Without you saying a word an infant will begin to watch and imitate what you're doing without making sense of it.

This law of nature doesn't change as a child gets older. A young child will reach for the things you reach for and try to eat the things that you eat. Children are full of curiosity so if someone is saying one thing and doing another, the child will try what you say, but they will also try what you do. Why? Because they saw you do it. You are an image in their eye. They want to see whether what you say is better or if what you do is better. This is the only way children can understand why you're doing what you're doing, even though you say children shouldn't do it. This is where the saying, "monkey see, monkey do" comes from.

People are made to naturally follow what other people are doing. We're sheep. Sheep follow. This is the initial way of learning. It's also called influence.

Influence is why a parent will try to control what a child sees and is exposed to. The parent knows and understands how easy a child will follow another child into danger. It is the same with the Father up above. He knows how easy one of His children will follow someone else into danger. That's why the Father wants you to meditate on Him and His Word night and day. This keeps your eyes focused on the best thing possible for your journey; the images that are the Word either placed in the book or in your heart. The goal is to keep you focused on this path.

If you believe that the Most High wants you to go up to the top of Mount Sinai, hold a firm picture in your mind of you going up to Mount Sinai for the Most High and if it is truly His will, you will invariably end up on the top of Mount Sinai. This is not a "you may end up" this is a "you WILL end up" consistently where the Most High needs and wants you to be as long as you take steps forward.

> *Philippians 4:8-9*
> *8Finally, brethren,* **whatsoever things are true***, whatsoever things* are *honest, whatsoever things* are *just,* **whatsoever things are pure***, whatsoever things* are *lovely, whatsoever things* are *of good report;* **if there be any virtue, and if**

there be *any praise, think on these things.*

9 Those things, which ye have both learned, and received, **and heard, and seen in me, do: and the God of peace shall be with you.**

IMAGES

All that we have are images. Man was made in the image of the Most High. If this is so, what is an image? Each letter is an image. Words are different combinations of images that together portray or point to a larger image. There are three letters in the word "eye" that instantly put an image into one's mind. The most common image you will see when reading that word is a part of the human face. If I were to say the eye of the storm, you would see something that is seemingly different. So, if Christ is the Word and words are images, we must return to the Word to decide how we should present the images of ourselves.

> *Colossians 1:15-16a*
> *15 Who is the* **image of the invisible God, the firstborn** *of every creature:*
> *16 For by him were all things created, that are in heaven, and that are in earth, visible and invisible*

Christ is the logo of God. The word "image" in Greek is *logos*. That is the image we must hold in our minds eye when deciding who we will be. We hold the image of Christ and his ways in our mind because that is the example the Most High sent us to copy voluntarily. If you voluntarily hold this image in your mind, you will copy it and desire to conform to it involuntarily in the same way that you became thirsty when looking at a cold drink in an advertisement. This image that we hold is not the traditional Caucasian man that is portrayed throughout the world. This image that we hold should look much like ourselves because when we see ourselves doing right in our mind's eye, we will do right voluntarily or involuntarily. This is the beginning of creation of the new man. We are literally manifesting righteousness in ourselves just by picturing it. This image of righteousness held firmly in our mind's eye sets righteousness in motion in our lives. This is the rebirth of being born again. This is faith. This is the hope.

> *Ephesians 4:23-24*
> *23 And be **renewed in the spirit of your mind**;*
> *24 And that ye **put on the new man**, which after*
>   *God is created in righteousness and true holiness.*

Consistently envision and consistently work towards your goal which is your picture and the Most High will correct your errors. This picture or image is just the verification of you knowing where you are going. We are not only children of God; we are students of God. We are getting hands on experience serving under Him. He is watching and guiding us in our crafts. This is our apprenticeship. When a carpenter starts out building something, there is a blueprint. The carpenter follows the blueprint to completion and makes whatever adjustments are necessary. The image that we are holding fast to is that blueprint and we are being guided by the Master Carpenter.

This is faith actualized. If you are not using this method, life will seem to be grievous for you. If life is grievous, you're doing life wrong. This is one thing that I have learned which I believe the average son of the Most High has forgotten.

Hebrews 11:1
*1Now faith is the substance of **things hoped for,** **the evidence of things not seen.***

GUARD YOUR IMAGE

Be mindful of what images are occupying your mind because you only have one mind. Be forceful with what goes into the image of your eye in the same way that you are forceful with what goes into your belly when fasting. This is how you strengthen your mind's eye. This is how you strengthen your faith and discipline. This is how you grow the muscle of faith; by using force. This spiritual force is the absence of physical action.

When fasting, you can either take actions to remove food out of the house, or on the contrary, you can just decide not to move at all. This means don't touch the food. Stay still. Don't lift your hand to your mouth. Stay still. Don't swallow. Stay still. This is practice for when you see sweet water that is not yours, but the voice of the adversary tells you to take that sweet water. Fasting is practice against the voice of the flesh. You do nothing. You just stay still. This voice is the voice of folly mentioned in Proverbs 9 below. When you strengthen your muscle of faith in this way, the image of the sweet water that you see can't rouse you to act on temptation.

Proverbs 9:16-18
*16Whoso is simple, let him turn in hither: and as for him that wanteth understanding, **she saith to him,***
*17**Stolen waters are sweet**, and bread eaten in secret is pleasant.*
*18But he knoweth not that **the dead are there**; and that her guests are in the depths of hell.*

GARRETT JACKSON

THE DUMB EYE

In the same way that companies make billboards and commercials to put the images of items and services in front of your eyes that they want you to consume, you should make your own internal billboards and commercials for your mind's eye that the Most High wants you to consume or act on. Make sure to run these Holy Spirit inspired internal ads every hour on the hour just as advertisers do for their products. Just as the masses are obedient to Nike and Hennessy ads, you too will become obedient to the righteous internal ads of the Word (images) that you create. This mind's eye doesn't have an IQ. It's a dumb eye, not a smart one, and it will be influenced by whatever is put in front of it. This is why vision boards work. Will you choose what you behold in your mind's eye or let the world that wants you to consume dictate what is in your mind?

> Instruction: Avoid the appearance of evil because we don't want to be contra to the call of the Most High. It makes the good that we are doing, vain. Remain aware of how you look to others at all times. Don't be a reflection of evil in someone else's eye.

9
HEART'S DESIRE

Remember that wherever your eye (light) is focused is where you will walk. It is way easier to keep your focus on your heart's desire because it is something that you truly want. You can't walk in two different directions at the same time so you must start with a plan. This plan that you start with will be your plan and not the Most High's plan. In actuality, it's most likely going to be a very bad plan and that's okay. Don't think that your first plan is going to be perfect and is going to go exactly how you expect it to go. A plan is simply a list of steps that you intend to take now or in the future.

> Proverbs 16:9
> 9 A man's **heart deviseth his way**: but the **LORD directeth his steps**.

When speaking to the Most High, be exact as possible in requesting what your heart devises while executing your plan. The voice of the Spirit will give you instructions with a heavenly end, but you must still ask for what you want and make your requests known. Be open to a change in plan and guidance from the Spirit because there is a better plan at work than the one that you have come up with. You must take each step mindfully and figure out where to place your feet. While doing this, Christ will light your path. He is the lamp. He will create a way. He will open a door, but you must knock.

> *Psalm 119:105*
> *105 Thy **word** is a **lamp** unto my feet, and a **light** unto my **path**.*

In Psalm 119, your feet must be moving in order for you to have a path. You don't need a light to stand still. Everything that was good for me that I have asked for with all my heart while being obedient, I have received. Your path is so complex that the Holy Spirit cannot give it to you completely at once, so She leads you with breadcrumbs.

There are people that you have to meet that you haven't met yet. There are places that you have to be that you have never heard of. There are institutions that you need to engage with that don't exist yet. If the Holy Spirit tried to tell you everything that you needed to do it wouldn't make sense, so She leads you little by little as you are ready. You confessing with your mouth is confirmation that you are ready for the next step. This confirms that you and the Most High are on the same page. "Page of what?" you may ask. The Word. The Most High already knows that your spirit is aligned with the Holy Spirit but is your flesh? This is why confession with the tongue is so important.

> *Proverbs 16:1-3*
> *1 The **preparations of the heart** in man, and the **answer of the tongue**, is from the LORD.*

*2All the ways of a man are clean in his own eyes; but
the **LORD weigheth the spirits**.
3**Commit thy works** unto the LORD, and **thy
thoughts shall be established**.*

HOW DO YOU ASK IN EARNEST?

When you don't know what to ask for or aren't capable of asking, the things that you need and want will be cried out for. This comes not by trying to pray cool (stylishly) but by praying as humbly, submissively, and lowly as possible. You must really desire the Most High. We are usually not praying with enough internal passion. I'm not talking about external passion like yelling your prayers, praying loudly, or praying theatrically. There is something that has to come from within. The process of asking is in Jeremiah. You don't just ask with your mouth; you ask with everything that you have.

*Jeremiah 29:12-14
12Then shall ye **call upon me**, and ye shall go and
pray unto me, and **I will hearken** unto you.
13**And ye shall seek me, and find me, when ye
shall search for me with all your heart**.
14And **I will be found of you**, saith the LORD:
and I will turn away your captivity, and I will
gather you from all the nations, and from all the
places whither I have driven you, saith the
LORD; and I will bring you again into the place
whence I caused you to be carried away captive.*

This internal place that your prayer must come from is similar to the place that you feel when you witness a gross injustice, and there's nothing that you can do about it. This same amount or level of pent-up emotion and desire to make whatever injustice that just happened, unhappen, must be directed toward the Most High. He is the only one that can fix or heal the situation.

When you get to this point in your life or to a point that you feel like you can't bear it anymore, you'll notice that your prayers start working. It's when you're at your lowest that prayer works the most. That's because we can't go any lower and your prayers are truly coming from the heart. Your situation has humbled you and made you submissive. So now, you actually mean what you say.

In hard times, those who are children of the Father become fervent and those who aren't are drawn away. Why do we let it get to this point? Why do we have to be made submissive through our situation or through chastisement? Let's submit voluntarily right now and cry out.

THE CRYING OUT

Crying out is not a sound. It's internal. What leads me to say that crying out is internal? When Abel endured a gross injustice the voice of his blood cried out to the Most High. When he couldn't pray and call out for help anymore, the voice of his blood cried out. The crying out of Abel occurred after Cain killed Abel.

> *Genesis 4:10*
> *10And he said, What hast thou done? the **voice of thy brother's blood crieth** unto me from the ground.*

In Sodom and Gomorrah, the angels came to destroy the land because of the cries. There were gross injustices taking place and the cries began to reach the Heavens. The Most

High clearly said that He went down to go investigate what was going on in Sodom.

> *Genesis 18:20-21*
> *20 And the LORD said,* **Because the cry of Sodom and Gomorrah is great,** *and because their sin is very grievous;*
> *21* **I will go down now, and see** *whether they have done altogether according to the cry of it, which is come unto me; and* ***if not, I will know.***

We assume that the Most High knows everything and He does but how and when is beyond our understanding. Even though the Most High knows what is best for you, you still have a will and a desire. Your prayers need to be cried out.

WHAT IS GIVEN VS DESIRED

If you never get anything that you initially desire and you only get what the Most High knows that you need, can or will you truly be happy? You may seek perfection, but you only appreciate perfection because you had the opportunity to experience your own imperfection of desires. It's almost like you got the girl that you wanted and it turned out bad. Then eventually, you got the girl that the Most High had for you, and she turned out to be what you needed. If the Most High gave you the perfect girl first, you may still be thinking about the imperfect girl in the back of your mind. This is most people, not everybody.

The Most High ultimately gives you what you need, but along the way, He also allows you some of the things that you want but may not be best for you. So, be careful what you ask for. Through these experiences and acquisitions you will/should eventually see that everything that glitters isn't gold, but even when it is gold (man's desires), the difference is that the Most High knows about the "GOOD" gold.

> *Genesis 2:11-12*
> *11 The name of the first is Pison: that is it which compasseth the whole land of Havilah, where there is gold;*
> *12 And* **the gold of that land is good: there is bdellium and the onyx stone.**

Do we settle for the regular gold or are we patient enough to wait for the good gold? Are we willing to take the time to seek the good gold? Many times in my life I have found regular gold, but I can see where I overlooked the good gold in hindsight. I think back and say to myself, "I passed up on what was really good for me." Primarily because I didn't know what was really good for me. I only knew what the world said was good for me.

THIS IS an example of an exact order:

Father, I see that the Holy Spirit has shown me that you want me to be a chef. This will provide me with the opportunity to feed those that have and those that don't. I don't know where to start, but your enlightenment and help is greatly appreciated.

NOW, meditate (think) on the task/goal that the Holy Spirit has given you. If you don't know how to, start thinking about the beginning of you becoming a chef. Then start thinking about the end and how it will be when you are a chef. Thank the Father for everything that you see in your meditation and request for knowledge, wisdom, and understanding. Since you believe that He wants you to be a chef, picture the place that you will be cooking in because every chef needs a kitchen. From there, picture the ingredients that you will be using. Picture what type of food you will be making. This will tell you what type of restaurant you will open.

Picture what type of pots and pans you'll be cooking with. Picture what type of stove you'll be cooking on. This will tell you what type of hardware to acquire. How many people do you see working around you in the kitchen? Is there a sous chef? Are there assistants? Are there waiters? Or is it a short order kitchen? This will tell you the size and capacity needed for the restaurant.

Now, picture walking into this restaurant that you're going to open up for the Most High. How does it look? Is it brick? Is it stucco? Is it standalone? Write everything that you see. Anything that you don't understand or don't know the answer to, research. Research, research, research. This is where part of the knowledge comes from and the Most High/Holy Spirit is where the wisdom and understanding come from.

Instruction: You have just started the beginning of your business plan. The things that you saw in the restaurant including the restaurant are what you should include in your plan to acquire. Start at the end and continue to go further and further back towards the present until you get to now/the start. So, the last thing that you should envision is yourself dressed and walking out of the door to start the plan. Now with everything that you have written down, bring it before the Most High. Ask Him to sanctify your plan. Ask Him to lead you and guide you. This is the way for you to achieve success for the Most High. Once you've brought it to the Most High, keep thine eye single and make this your primary vision/mission. Handle periphery items as they come and as you must but never go a day without pondering or thinking on what the Most High has for you primarily.

This technique can be applied to anything the Most High has for you to do, no matter how great or how simple the task. If the task is to get in shape, picture yourself in shape. Observe what muscles you see toned and defined. Then look up workouts that tone and define those muscles. Look up diets that also lead to those muscles being toned and defined. When you see those muscles toned and defined, what kind of gym do you see? Are you at the gym or at home? Do you have the equipment you need at home? If not, get the equipment. If you don't have the resources to get the equipment, get the resources, and so on, and so on. Even though this is a simple task, still bring it before the Most High and ask for His blessing.

Check within yourself to determine if you want the things that you want because the world says they are good or if these things are good because the Most High deems them good and valuable. After this, realign yourself and your plan with the Most High and not the world.

10

DOMINION THROUGH ORDER

Jeremiah 7:13
*13And now, because **ye have done all these works**, **saith** the **LORD**, and **I spake unto you**, rising up early and **speaking, but ye heard not**; and **I called you**, but ye answered not*

Dominion comes with a sense of urgency and is relative to time. When the Comforter speaks to you, it is not a suggestion. It is a command. Commands demand action so actions are required of you. When you realize and fully digest this, your life will change.

Be mindful at all times, because it is easy to forget that the Comforter may be speaking to you to act upon the good. The voice of the Comforter is not merely a feature of the Most High. For you, it is the main thing. This is the spirit of the Most High. If the Most High was a phone, the voice of the Spirit wouldn't be a fingerprint sensor or a camera. The voice of the Spirit is more akin to the operating system of the phone. If the Most High was an iPhone, the Spirit would be iOS. The Comforter is front and center for how the Most High communicates with us today.

Gone are the days of the Ephod, the Ark, and the Urim and the Thummim. What we have now is direct communication through the Spirit that dwells in our hearts. If the heart is really the mind, the law that is written in our mind will come across as thoughts. Your thoughts are heard in your mind/heart as a voice. You can't even think a thought without the silent inaudible voice of a thought.

Throughout life and even while reading this book, pay attention to your thoughts and set them in order. Pay attention to the words running through your mind. Pay special attention to the words, sentences and thoughts that keep reoccurring. You will hear many thoughts come across your mind, but there are certain thoughts that lead to more life. There are certain thoughts that lead to prosperity. There are certain thoughts that lead to health. There are certain thoughts that lead to righteousness and justice. These are from the Comforter.

The thoughts of doubt, fear of trying, destruction, transgression, hate, and everything else that is against you lead to death. These are from the adversary and the flesh. The more that you observe thoughts, the more you'll understand that these involuntary thoughts, positive and negative, are not yours at all.

All of the thoughts that you are hearing in your mind are actually darts being thrown across a battlefield and that battlefield is your mind. As you try to listen, you'll notice that the thoughts stop or slow down for a time because your mind (eye) has become single in observing. The reason why the thoughts stopped is because you the non-thinker started to observe them closely. If they were your thoughts, why would they flee from your focused presence and why can't you make them restart where they left off?

There are two opposing sides. You will realize that you have the power to clear your mind temporarily but not stop your brain from thinking totally. If these were your thoughts, you would be able to completely shut them off. If these were your thoughts, you would be able to come up with good thoughts and genius ideas at will, but the fact of the matter is, you don't come up with genius ideas everyday or have eureka moments at will because these aren't your thoughts at all. These thoughts come when you are ready to receive them. You must graduate to the next level of thought by setting your current thoughts in order, thus dominating them. Set your thoughts in order, the same way that you set your room in order.

The good thoughts are thoughts from the source of wisdom, the Holy Spirit. This is the same wisdom that Solomon was endowed with. We are of that lineage. We have the same access to the Comforter. Under your control, you have thoughts of a man/flesh and can make man level thoughts at will because you are a man, but from time to time, you receive divine thoughts that are sent from the Most High through the Holy Spirit.

You are granted these thoughts from the Most High and the Most High should be given credit. These are the thoughts that will lead you to and through the path of the strait and narrow most expeditiously. These thoughts come to you the same way that they came to Daniel. King Nebuchadnezzar asked him to translate a dream that even he (Nebuchadnezzar) couldn't remember. Daniel prayed for the proper thoughts and received the proper interpretation from the Most High. These interpretations were not his thoughts or dreams. That's why he had to pray for it. He recognized this and gave credit where credit was due.

> *Daniel 2:19-20*
> *19 **Then was the secret revealed unto Daniel** in a night vision. Then Daniel blessed the God of heaven.*
> *20 Daniel **answered and said**, Blessed be the name of God for ever and ever: **for wisdom and might are his**:*

THOUGHTS OF THE PAST

After you identify good thoughts, begin to categorize all of the thoughts and ideas. Righteous thoughts from the Spirit that deal with the past always involve learning from past experiences. Thoughts from the adversary that deal with the past always include a negative emotion, such as regret, nostalgia, reminiscing (longing), and sadness. If you want to detach yourself from the thoughts of the past write them down. Write down what you've learned as a piece of knowledge to grow from and never return back to these thoughts voluntarily once you've grown. If you return back to that thought involuntarily, mark it as a positive thought and then think about what you've learned again. There's a reason why you've returned to this thought. There must be something to gain or the Spirit is encouraging you by reminding you of what you've learned.

When your mind repeatedly returns back to a negative thought, it can be due to a lack of nutrition or a temporary deficit of the body. When everything is perceived to be great in life, we're not thinking about the past. We're focused on making new memories. It is when things aren't so great that we lose what little control we have over our minds. Our minds have the tendency to think in stress patterns. When your brain isn't handling stress correctly, it returns back to other stressful events that provide more negative thoughts. It's a snowball effect.

When you're going through a hard time in life, many times you reflect on other bad things, and you develop a victim mindset, but this is most likely due to the fact that your brain isn't processing cortisol correctly. There are things like folic acid and ashwagandha that help your body and mind deal with stress and depression. Many of us are suffering from depression because we are malnourished and a major symptom of suffering from depression is focusing on the past too much. Our bodies don't have the proper nutrition to combat stress. In your free time, look up foods and nutrients that fight stress.

THOUGHTS OF THE PRESENT

Righteous thoughts that deal with the present and the future are your instructions from the Holy Spirit. These things should be written down as well and placed on your roadmap for the strait and narrow as waypoints. Things that you cannot get done today should be in the category of planning and preparation, but outside of that, much dwelling on these things isn't necessary. There is surely something that you are doing today that requires your full attention and your mind's power. Ultimately, what you're doing today is something that you received from the Spirit on one of your yesterdays. Very soon the thought that you received on one of the yesterdays, but was for the future, will be ripe for today.

Negative thoughts from the adversary regarding the future are all based in fear. It's primarily fear of the unknown. What the Most High God has for you, it is for you, so you can receive it with a solemn spirit and no fear. What He has given, no man can take away. Even if they take away all your physical possessions, there should still be no fear. If there is, you don't understand what He truly gave you.

We fear failure of the future. We fear what people will say about what we will do in the future. We fear that we are not doing the right thing today, so the future will be bad. Through faith we must still move forward. You will soon realize that what the Most High has in store for us in the future is so great that if we knew everything now, we would quit from the weight of the responsibility. This is similar to how Solomon quivered at the thought of the responsibility of running the great kingdom that David built. He only needed one thing to be successful and that is wisdom and understanding from the Most High. That's the Voice.

Don't write down negative thoughts regarding the future from the adversary; just ignore them. There's already enough fear in trying to execute one of the Father's genius ideas because these divine ideas aren't small ideas, they are unimaginably great ideas.

A CALL TO ACTION

Where do your instructions from the Voice of the Most High lead? Envision where the Most High has told you to go. Envision the instructions He's already given you. If you have no instructions after you've categorized and ordered your thoughts, act on the first thought that you can for the Most High regarding righteousness, health, and prosperity.

If you need help hearing the voice of the Most High, you have to start small. Set aside a day to only do what the Spirit has told you to do. The Spirit will never go overboard because the Most High knows what you can bear and His work is not grievous. The less discipline and the less together your life is, the simpler your instruction will be. Before you get the complex parts of your life together, you have to start with the basic parts of your life. This may be something as simple as brushing your teeth, washing your clothes, or cutting the grass.

Why would the Most High start here? It's because you and everything around you are representations of Him the moment you profess His name. Be prepared to be able to present yourself and everything under your control and dominion as a perfect sacrifice and representation of the Most High.

Don't show up to the Shabbat or the job interview with a mustard stain on your shirt. There's always someone watching you. If you can be without blemish, be without blemish. Do your best. Give the Most High your best. If you wouldn't go on a date with a mustard stain, don't show up for the bridegroom with a mustard stain.

As you move toward the instruction the Most High has given you, with faith, picture the instructions already being done. Renew this picture in your mind daily, hourly, and even by the minute if need be. Do everything you can and nothing more than that. You can't force it. You have to let the objective come to you.

Your current job after you've done all you can, is only to visualize in a praying and meditating manner or posture. You have to let the Most High bring it to you when you're ready. The more you chase it, the further away it will be. Anything you chase, has to be running away or else you would just walk up and claim it. In the meantime, just prepare yourself for the task that you believe the Father has for you so that you are ready when the time approaches.

I know exactly when you'll receive what the Most High has for you. When is that? It's when you're ready. When you're ready is when you're patient enough and prepared enough. If you're not patient enough for the next level in your life, it means you're rushing. If you're rushing through this level to get to the next level that you're envisioning, then you're going to rush through the next level of your life as well.

Relax, you just got here. You don't want your life to become about the next level. It should be about where you are now and enjoying the blessings and the things that the Most High has given you while preparing and improving yourself for whatever is next. Don't let your life only become about getting to the next level. Give gratitude and thanksgiving for your current position.

IGNORANCE OF THE COMFORTER'S VOICE

As much as this is about hearing and listening to the Most High's voice with purpose, it is also about not ignoring the Most High's voice by accident. We are so far from the Most High right now that we have forgotten His voice. The assignments and instructions may seem easy and simple today, but it is only so that we are able to grow so familiar with His voice that all doubt is removed regarding who is speaking to us. If the Voice told you right now to sacrifice your child, who would you think it was? I would think it was the devil too, but somehow Abraham knew that it was the Most High. This is how familiar we must be with the voice of the Most High. This is how much faith and trust we must have in Him. This is the pinnacle of obedience.

> *Genesis 22:1-2*
> 1*And it came to pass after these things, that God did tempt Abraham, and said* unto him, Abraham: and he said, Behold, *here I am.*
> 2*And he said, Take now thy son, thine*

***only* son *Isaac, whom thou lovest,** and get thee into the land of Moriah; and offer him there **for a burnt offering** upon one of the mountains which I will tell thee of.*

It clearly says where these instructions came from.

11
PLOT ARMOR

Move like you have on plot armor.

The appearance of lawlessness has the world scared into a stupor. Be mindful that this appearance is only a deception. Media is controlled by the lawless, so the images of lawlessness are magnified. Magnification is the same as glorification. Don't be deceived by false magnification. The world still belongs to the Most High, and you still have dominion.

All images are false images. Every year new cameras and camera phones are released to show you an improved depiction of what is really there in the photo. Last year's camera couldn't capture it and this year's camera can't either. What is truly there can never be captured.

In the same way a person can't show you who they fully and truly are in person or in an image, media also can't show you what the world is fully through an image. It is impossible to know the world through a screen. People have to be experienced and so does the world. Only the Father searcheth the reigns and fully understands your ways and who you are. Do your ways match His way, which is the way of Christ?

THE KNOWING

Knowing what is a lie unveils the truth. You don't have to know the truth, it just is. The truth can seem inconsistent and be true. A lie can be perfectly consistent and still be a lie. Media is manipulative.

In any mainstream movie, tv show or novel, you know that the main character (MC) cannot die early on for the shenanigans to continue. For longevity's sake, the plot always has to make a way for the MC to survive, overcome, or grow, even during times of downfall. The suspense can only build to a certain point for a seasoned show watcher because after watching so many different shows, a seasoned viewer can almost see where the writer is leaving an opening for the MC to be delivered. This opening is called plot armor.

The plot protects the MC until the story ends or has developed enough for another potential MC. Rarely do you see a MC die within the first season, so any danger that you see the MC in, can be safely assumed to only be superficial. Early on in the show, you're reassured by all of your experiences of watching tv and movies that this character can't and won't die, but that's only if the authors know what's good for them. This reassurance is called plot faith.

The Most High is the author of life's story of truth. Every story is a journey. If you're reading this, chances are very high that you are an MC. And guess what? You have plot armor. This armor is what comes with being a child of the Most High.

> *Ephesians 6:10-17*
> *10 Finally, my brethren, **be strong in the Lord**, and **in the power of his might**.*
> *11 Put on the whole **armour of God**, that ye may be able **to stand against the wiles of the devil**.*
> *12 For we wrestle not against flesh and blood, but against principalities, against powers, against the rulers of the darkness of this world, against spiritual wickedness in high places.*
> *13 Wherefore take unto you the whole **armour of God**, that ye may be able **to withstand in the evil day**, and having done all, to stand.*
> *14 Stand therefore, having your loins girt about with truth, and having on the breastplate of righteousness;*
> *15 And your feet shod with the preparation of the gospel of peace;*
> *16 Above all, taking the shield of faith, wherewith ye shall be able to quench all the fiery darts of the wicked.*
> *17 And take the helmet of salvation, and **the sword of the Spirit, which is the word of God**:*

I am obligated to give you this warning. If the Most High doesn't like where your story is heading, your plot armor can and will be removed at any time. You as the MC will be replaced and your story will change genres. It will turn from a hero-adventure story into a drama-tragedy, or maybe even an horror.

> *Proverbs 1:24-28*
> *24 Because **I have called, and ye refused**; I have stretched out my hand, and no man regarded;*

> *25 But ye have set at nought all my counsel, and would none of my reproof:*
> *26 **I also will laugh at your calamity**; I will mock when your fear cometh;*
> *27 When your fear cometh as desolation, and your destruction cometh as a whirlwind; when distress and anguish cometh upon you.*
> *28 Then shall **they call upon me**, but **I will not answer**; they **shall seek** me early, but **they shall not find** me:*

Yes, you are an integral part of the story, but there's no one begging you to play any role that you're not willing to play. There's a story waiting to be lived and told through your gifts. Stephen was willing to tell the story of truth. Are you willing to tell it? Let's see how Stephen used his gift.

After the telling of this story, Stephen was stoned. This plot armor is durable enough to carry you until you complete your purpose. Stephen completed his purpose using his armor, but many of us are not using our plot armor at all. It is because we don't trust in the Most High with all of our heart. Many of us don't believe that we will be delivered for His name's sake and for the sake of the Most High's story. You have the same capability of doing incredible wonders and miracles as well. I want you to take a break to read the full chapter of Acts 7. Hold the story that Stephen told as a marker of what truth sounds like.

> *Acts 6:8,10 (Stephen's Gift Exhibited)*
> *8 **And Stephen, full of faith and power**, did great wonders and miracles among the people.*
> *10 And **they were not able to resist the wisdom and the spirit by which he spake**.*

Your story stands next to the stories mentioned; as equal and as tall. Why? Because the story of your life is happening right now. It's real and it's true. Our forefathers are in the book now, but you too will be there soon. In Revelation 20, it says that on judgement day the story of your life will be read to determine your entrance into the Kingdom. Are you a hero or a villain? An MC or an NPC (bot)?

Only central characters in the Most High's plot will have plot armor. How do you become a central character in the Most High's plot? By becoming one of the main people willing to take action in the plot. By this, you become one of His children. You can't die if, without you the plot can't go on. We were all made for a purpose and if you are intent on doing your purpose, you won't leave the plot until your purpose is done. Now, live life accordingly.

> Revelation 20:12
> 12 And I saw the dead, small and great, stand before God; **and the books were opened: and another book was opened, which is the book of life**: and the dead were judged out of those things which were written in the books, **according to their works**.

12
CONTINUAL SACRIFICE

If you are struggling to find your dominion, you may be in need of a continual sacrifice. A continual sacrifice is the giving up of something that is hindering you, spiritually or physically, that you participate in frequently but is not expedient to the ways of the Most High. When small hindrances keep occurring they are usually warnings. Examine your ways and consult the Father. This is the way.

> Psalm 119:9-12
> 9 The *fear of the LORD* **is** *clean*, *enduring for ever: the* **judgments** *of the LORD* are *true* and *righteous altogether.*
> 10 *More to be desired* are they *than gold, yea, than much fine gold: sweeter also than honey and the honeycomb.*
> 11 *Moreover* **by them is thy servant warned***:* and *in keeping of them* there is *great reward.*
> 12 **Who can understand** **his** *errors? cleanse thou me from* **secret faults***.*

In ancient times, continual sacrifices are what were given for the so-called "light" sins. They are also intended for the secret faults that David speaks of above. At certain points in the Bible, someone would say in a prayer something to the effect of, Father forgive me for the sins that I don't know I have committed or they might say, forgive me for something that I did in the heat of the moment but now feel conviction for. These are usually sins that most people don't acknowledge or are ignorant of.

The only way that something could be done without being completely sure it was a sin is if, the act committed wasn't directly addressed in the law. This would make it a grey sin or something that sort of blurs the line of a sin. Thus, people would give sacrifices daily or weekly just in case something that they were doing was wrong.

Many times these sins are attached to a habit or an addiction. It is all relative. Someone who has had one drink, just had a drink but for someone who has been having a few drinks a day for the last three years and their liver is dying, is it a sin? This is what a continual sacrifice is designed for.

Job woke up daily and made sacrifices for his children just in case they were doing something wrong. These sacrifices were intended to nullify the sins of the children regardless of if the children were remorseful or not. In Job 1, we see how this worked out for his children and after the new covenant, these sacrifices are no longer accepted. The lack of love and remorse in the people's hearts combined with these "grey" sins are what diminish dominion.

While committing these types of sin, you will receive conviction once the act is complete. You will also face chastisement (warnings) from the Most High in various ways. It will feel like for some reason, you just can't get your life fully on track or get things to turn out the way that you want them to. This is because the Most High wants you to turn toward

Him completely so that you can reach your maximum potential for Him.

I refer to this maximum potential as the pinnacle of dominion. During the pinnacle of dominion, one may feel as if they can't make a mistake or make a bad decision. Everything you do or say seems to just work. This is because you are making decisions in your life for the benefit of the Most High and He wants you to win.

In order for us to truly win, our lives must be a continual sacrifice within a sacrifice. Through dedication to the Most High, we sacrifice our lives to be committed to Him. Then when the parts of our lives develop that can hinder our journey with the Most High, we also sacrifice those pieces of our lives. We must first circumcise our hearts and then further circumcise our lives. Cutting away the unneeded and the things that hinder is our continual sacrifice.

SACRIFICE SETS ORDER

If you've sacrificed all potential sin in your life and you still feel like something is wrong or missing, sacrifice resources next. The love of money or the dependence on money and not the Most High is a hidden sin and can throw off your balance of dominion on the Earth. Your dominion should not be dependent upon money.

Everything must be done in order. Putting priority on something sets an order of importance so don't be financially tempted to put yourself before the building of the kingdom and the Most High. The Most High has always been about order, thus He requires Himself to be the top priority. This is what it means when the Bible says that the Most High God is a jealous god. He's jealous because He wants to come first and be exhorted.

Jeremiah 25:6-7

*6And **go not after other gods** to serve them, and to worship them, and provoke me not to anger with the works of your hands; **and I will do you no hurt.***

*7**Yet ye have not hearkened unto me,** saith the LORD; that ye might provoke me to anger with the works of your hands to your own hurt.*

Exodus 22:20

20He that sacrificeth unto any god, save unto the LORD only, he shall be utterly destroyed.

A tithe is a sacrifice. When Cain gave his offering, he didn't prioritize the Most High. Cain didn't give the Most High his firstlings; his best. Thus, his offering was not accepted. Able gave the Most High his best and his first, and the Father was pleased. So, even tithes, the giving of your first tenth, shows that you have priority for the Most High. This life, this sacrifice is about priority for the Most High.

Instruction: If you find yourself being held back, figure out what your continual sacrifice needs to be. Consult your spirit and the Holy Spirit deeply because these sacrifices are tailor made for you. It might feel like it's impossible to overcome and make this sacrifice, but as sure as the sun will rise in the morning, it is possible. We are more than conquerors. We are sons of the Most High God.

PART TWO

13

THE LUXURIOUS CALLING

To be what He intended requires awareness.

Do we fully understand what the Most High has made us to do? On this journey, the Father will put us in positions to work for Him, but sometimes we don't see what He has called us to do as an occupation. This oversight can be for many reasons, but the most frequent reason is that we lack awareness of the Voice calling us.

If you have the opportunity to follow through fully in your calling, it is the most luxurious thing that you can do. Luxury is all about having a choice and there is no greater choice than this one. Being able to go where the Most High wants you to go is way more luxurious than being able to go where you want to go.

GARRETT JACKSON

KNOWLEDGE IS A LUXURY

Reading is the most underrated luxury at your disposal. It requires your most limited resource, which is time. Not everyone has the luxury to set aside two hours to read. More importantly, not everyone has the discipline to dedicate two hours to read. Does this mean that luxury requires discipline?

In whatever profession that you want to pursue for the Most High, learning is going to be required and many times this will require reading. When you are reading to grow, the materials you read are written by someone that is very knowledgeable, experienced, or an expert. It is literally the equivalent of getting trained from a master in a subject and this training is a luxury.

When a person goes to school to get a medical or law degree, they are not tested on the expertise of the teacher, they are tested on the expertise of the authors of the books. What is on the test comes from the university approved books. This means that if you read, memorize, and understand the materials in the books approved, you will have the same expertise as the medical or law school graduate. No, you will not have the degree, but you will have the expertise and this goes for any subject. So, if you want to change the knowledge level of your gift from hobby level to expert, consult an expert whether that be in person or through books.

The best thing about the luxury of knowledge through reading is that it can be done anywhere. You can learn in a bedroom or a classroom. You can learn in a forest or on a beach. You can even learn at work or on vacation. No matter where you are, the luxury of learning through reading never ceases. The content will always be the content.

There are buildings called libraries that are full of these luxurious items called books. The libraries even let you check out these capsules of expert knowledge for free and take them to whatever destination that you desire. The only requirement is that you bring back each capsule of knowledge in the same condition that you checked it out in. The number one rule of the library is to be quiet and respectful because peace is required at all times. We actually have no excuse for not being experts in any area of interest that we desire. I recommend that the first book or subject that you become an expert in be the Bible.

GIFT OR HOBBY

Whatever your gift is you will have a natural inclination towards it. We may love and enjoy what we do so much that we see it as a hobby and don't take it seriously. The Father created each and every one of us for different purposes, so it only makes sense that you would have a natural inclination or desire for the thing/purpose that He created you to do. We tend to see other people doing the thing that we consider to be our hobby at a higher professional level and think less of ourselves because others are already so skilled and profitable at the craft. It may even look like others were born to do it and that they have a natural talent for it, but trust me, it's hard to determine the difference between what's talent and what's hard work from the outside looking in.

Someone who has played music their whole life will look naturally gifted to someone seeing them perform for the first time at the age of 28 because we typically only see the end result, which is the performance. Behind the scenes there has been grueling hours of practice, preparation, and rehearsing. The good thing is that the hours are only grueling when you're not enjoying what you're doing.

The Most High made you for your purpose so take your time and be consistent. Focus on appreciating the craft and getting better. The only reason professionals are better than us at a craft is because they take it seriously and have put in more work. They work on their craft daily like it's a job with intention and purpose. We need to work daily as well but with a different intention. While you're working on your craft remember, it's not for you or an audience, it's for the Father. You're just there for the ride. This craft is what will give you the opportunity to glorify and exalt the name of the Most High God. Ultimately, glorifying Him is the true purpose and calling of all His children.

MY EXPERIENCE WITH INSTRUCTIONS

Regarding your calling, your instructions will hit you more like when a great or genius idea comes to your mind/heart. It's the type of idea that when you hear it, it's so good or in tune with what you want to do that natural motivation and excitement is built into the idea. Our lives really should be about us hearing unbelievable ideas from the Spirit, executing those ideas, and then giving glory to the Father when credit is given to us or whenever we have the opportunity. This is what a fisherman's journey on the strait and narrow looks like on a macro basis.

> *Proverbs 1:8-9*
> **8*My son, hear the instruction of thy father,***
> ***and forsake not the law of thy mother****:*
> *9For they shall be an ornament of grace unto thy head, and chains about thy neck.*

If we are freemen, we must ask the Father what positions He has available for us to work. If He says author, get to writing. You may sit down one day and only receive 1-4 pages of writing for the entire 24 hours or you may only receive 10 words. Know that this is okay, because working for the Father is not grievous. At a traditional 9 to 5 job, you are trained to be doing something every second of the day, and when there is nothing left to do, you learn to look like there is something to do by appearing busy. This is not so with the Father. He gives us time to think and ponder. More importantly, He gives us time to listen for the Comforter to make sure we are still headed down the correct path.

Oftentimes, we take our calling so lightly that we don't see it as a job or an assignment. We will literally be in the middle of doing something related to our purpose and put it down to do the so-called "real work". An aspiring carpenter destined to build homes and solve the housing crisis will put down his so-called side project (his calling) and say, "let me go do some real work," and then clock-in at a full-time work from home telemarketing job. All of this is done while being unaware of his calling to change the world. In this situation, the carpentry is not currently making money so there is little respect for it.

It is also important to remember to start your transformation for the Most High in the job that is your current position. If we do our current jobs in a certain manner, by listening to the voice of the Most High daily and working as if we're working directly for the Most High, we will soon become freemen. This is the same thing that happened to Joseph when he was a slave. While working in a certain manner for the Most High under the pharaoh, he was eventually promoted over the kingdom. Promotion lies in the hands of the Most High. Your calling is what will feed you ultimately and eternally.

> *1 Corinthians 7:21-24*
> *21**Art thou called being a servant?** care not for it: but **if thou mayest be made free, use it rather**.*
> *22For he that is **called in the Lord**, being a servant, **is the Lord's freeman**: likewise also he that is called, being free, is Christ's servant.*
> *23Ye are bought with a price; **be not ye the servants of men**.*
> *24**Brethren, let every man, wherein he is called, therein abide with God**.*

While writing this book, the thought of washing my car or something else menial could flash across my mind. If I were to abandon the Most High's task for my own personal tasks, I would not be taking the position of author as serious as a typical job. You usually can't leave work in the middle of the day to wash your car. It's almost like there was no respect for the work because the work wasn't grievous and the words of the book came without much effort. I had to remember that our words and talents all come from up above, so treat your new occupation as such. We have been conditioned to only respect work that's hard on the back and mind or what's given to us by a slave master. We need to change that mindset.

> *Matthew 11:28-30*
> *28**Come unto me, all ye that labour and are heavy laden**, and **I will give you rest**.*
> *29**Take my yoke upon you**, and learn of me; for I am meek and lowly in heart: and **ye shall find rest unto your souls**.*
> *30For **my yoke is easy, and my burden is light**.*

At the end of the day when you are done working for the Father, you may feel like you haven't done much. This is because you were made for the Father's work given to you. It's not grievous. This is the type of work we must gravitate towards and complete. Christ was a carpenter, but did you ever read about him doing carpentry? No. The Greek word for carpenter is *teckton* which means builder. If you were paying attention, Christ was building the church.

> *Ephesians 2:19-22*
> *19 Now therefore ye are no more strangers and foreigners, but fellow citizens with the saints, and of the household of God;*
> *20 **And are built upon the foundation** of the apostles and prophets, <u>the Son of God</u>, **Christ himself being the chief corner stone;***
> *21 In whom all the building fitly framed together groweth unto an holy temple in the Lord:*
> *22 In whom ye also are builded together for an habitation of God through the Spirit.*

This is the kind of work the Father has available for us. He doesn't have any grievous positions. If you want that, go back into the world. Here there won't be anybody barking orders at you or whipping your back. The Father's salary and reward for you is eternal. Thus, His blessings are not always immediate. On this journey, the most grievous thing you will have to do is overcome your flesh.

Rarely do we take the Father's work seriously and rarely do we finish what we start for the Most High. This also includes me. I know this to be true because the world would look completely different. As of right now and as a nation, we are overcome by the cares of the world.

Mark 4:19
19 And **the cares of this world**, and the deceitfulness of **riches**, and the **lusts** of other things entering in, **choke the word**, and it becometh unfruitful.

Instruction: Our flesh driven desires get in the way of our purpose and make hearing the Comforter within us more difficult. The Word is the instructions/commands written in the book and within us. Take your position in the Father's workforce as serious as you take your job in the world.

14
GIFTS AND ABILITIES

The work of the Most High is not grievous, so if life is feeling grievous or overbearing, it is probably because you're not using your gift, ignoring your calling, or being disobedient (absence of a continual sacrifice). You will find that when you are fully in your proper role, position, or occupation and using your gift, your strongest effort and attention aren't required because the gig comes naturally. It's not a struggle to stay focused because you can already see what to do next. You were given at least one special gift so if you focus your life around it, your life will just flow.

Figuring out the specifics regarding this gift is a journey within itself. Your gift is usually going to be something that you like to do for free, but people insist on paying you for it or they can't believe that you are doing it for free. You do it for free because you were given this gift for free. Thus, it's not a burden to do. That's why it's called a gift and not a reward. If you had to put in 20,000 hours and spend a fortune on it, you would definitely be charging or at the very least, considering it.

A gift is a talent or knack that you can naturally do better than the average person without much additional effort. You either perform at a higher level than those with the same teaching and experience or you can perform in a way that can't be taught. You may even be able to do something that no one else can do. If you worked hard to attain this gift, it's not a gift. It would be the result of hard work that the Most High gave you the ability to pursue and receive. If that is the case, He gave you the opportunity to attain an ability and not necessarily a gift.

THE SIMPLICITY OF A GIFT

Gifts are a lot simpler than most people perceive them to be. For instance, a doctor or healer's gift isn't necessarily going to be healing. In modern medicine, a good healer may be someone who has great memory and recall. Healers memorize a lot of symptoms and the diseases associated with those symptoms, so when they see a patient, they ask first about their symptoms. Then from the symptoms, they come up with a list of diseases or issues that are plausible. After that, they test for each disease to figure out the patient's sickness.

Someone who has memorized all available medical material in a specific area is considered to be a good healer, but someone who has memorized all the material in multiple areas and has good recall would be regarded as a genius level doctor. Is the doctor's gift medicine or memory and recall? This same genius could have gone down an artistic path and be considered a great painter because they can memorize all of the useful painting techniques. After seeing a landscape, skyline or structure, they then have the gift to recall and include what they saw with great detail in the paintings. This same gift could make them a generational artist.

The simplicity of our gifts can make them hard to see. Another way that I can explain a gift is that it is an area that the Spirit has given a person more insight, understanding or awareness than the regular person. A child prodigy in piano seems to just understand the piano and how to play it more. It's almost as if the child can see, hear, and feel the piano and the music that it makes better than other children. I believe that these gifts are the Spirit unlocking that little extra something in our minds. How does a child know what to do next outside of hearing or seeing it? It's instinct. Many believe that instinct is from the flesh, but it is actually spiritual just like your conscience.

HARD WORK VS A GIFT

What I have found in my experience is that hard work and practice can't match the results of the Spirit working through you while using your gift. Hard work gets you to good, maybe even to great, but when the Holy Spirit is operating, you get results so amazing that you couldn't duplicate it again through hard work even if your life depended on it. Some people confuse this fleeting presence of the Spirit with luck or chance. The more in tune you become with the Comforter, the less fleeting She will seem.

Also know that your gift can be taken away if misused or if you make it too grievous by adding unnecessary work or the worry of the past and future regarding it. Our gift is us listening to the instructions (commandments) of the Most High while in motion. This motion will most likely be something that you enjoy because people usually enjoy doing things that they're good at. This is when you are at your best. This is when we are most victorious through Him.

When it comes to our gifts we tend to feel like our strongest effort and attention is needed, but when you really pay attention, you'll notice and soon know that your gift isn't yours at all; it's the Most High's. All gifts come from Him.

For some, their gifts can't be wielded at will. They have to wait on the Spirit because they can't premeditate the use of their gift. If you are out of alignment with the Most High, you may not even be able to access your gift at all. At times, one may only have enough access to get good or great results from the craft, skills, or gift that they have obtained through hard work. The gifted can feel the difference between the greatness of hard work and the immeasurable glory of Holy Spirit filled works when they are in motion. Be ye not fooled, the Father can even take away the results of your hard work.

> *James 1:17*
> *17**Every good gift and every perfect gift** is from above, and cometh down **from the Father of lights**, with whom is no variableness, neither shadow of turning.*

If you're putting all your effort into your gift, I will venture to say that a great part of your energy and effort is misplaced. This is because when God is working through you, no amount of human effort matters. Some may be deceived into thinking that they are special and that it's them or their hard work, but it's not. It's the Most High God working.

> *Galatians 6:3*
> *3For if a man think himself to be something, when he is nothing, **he deceiveth himself**.*

Most, if not all, of your effort needs to be focused on staying righteous and avoiding temptation. Your full focus is needed for the evil in the present. It is important to differentiate God given gifts from abilities early in your journey so that you will know where to place your effort and hard work. The largest amount of effort should be placed on your walk and staying aligned with the Most High. You will find that the more you stay upright, the more all other matters just seem to fall into place without much effort.

> Matthew 6:34
> 34 Take therefore **no thought for the morrow**: for the morrow shall take thought for the things of itself. **Sufficient unto the day** is **the evil thereof.**

The second most amount of effort will usually go towards your abilities because your abilities will require more time than gifts for you to become competent. An ability is a skill that you acquired to help shed light on your gift. It can also be a skill not related to your gift that you picked up randomly, but the random abilities should not be getting a large portion of your time. For instance, a rapper may have to learn some elements of music engineering to complete a song. If you're a singer, you may learn to play an instrument to help you write songs. In this instance, your gift would be singing, but your ability would be playing an instrument. If you're a tailor, you may have to learn the mechanics of a sewing machine so that you can fix it. Repairing sewing machines is one of your abilities and shouldn't become your main focus. Your gift is still being a tailor, unless the Spirit tells you otherwise. Sometimes we find our gift through trying different abilities.

I know this sounds somewhat counterintuitive but the least amount of time is probably going to go towards your gift because you're a natural; and you're a spiritual. To put it into context, imagine someone born with a body that is tailored toward playing tennis, but they decide to play football. This person will have to put in a lot more time (and effort) in the gym to build a football physique in comparison to someone that is born with a physique tailored toward playing football.

Our gifts are no different. Everything requires work, but you were born with a spiritual physique that is tailored for your gift. You were born with a strong foundation for your gift that requires less effort than it does for someone who is just attaining an ability.

These abilities are usually acquired to complement and accentuate your gifts, to bring them into fruition on a base level. Putting a large amount of energy into abilities is okay and only temporary until you can find your synergy (we'll discuss the synergy concept in a later chapter). In everything that you do for the Most High God, He still requires you to do it with all your heart, but the specialness of your performance comes from Him.

> *Mark 12:30*
> *30 And thou shalt* **love the Lord thy God with all thy heart**, *and with all thy soul, and with all thy mind,* **and with all thy strength**: *this* is *the first commandment.*

Because your full attention should be directed to the strait and narrow, the majority of your attention should be going towards the Most High, the Word, Charity, and keeping your eye as single as possible. If you focus on these things, God will handle the rest by giving you instruction and assistance through the voice of the Holy Spirit. Your gift will also be increased as needed for your assignment.

VAIN HORSEPOWER

I hear some people speak of this thing that they refer to as an "engine." Someone with a strong engine, sometimes called a motor, is someone that seems to never get tired. In sports if a person has a strong engine, this is referring to their ability to do a lot of reps at full force. It can also be looked at as how much energy and effort a person can output continually through individual instances night after night. For example, Kawhi Leonard and Joel Embiid would be considered low engine players who are inconsistent with either force or effort over time. While, Giannis Antetokounmpo and LeBron James would be considered high engine players because they appear to be giving max effort and force all the time. This same concept can be applied to many fields, especially entrepreneurs or commission-based workers. How much work salaried employees (workers) get done is typically determined by the slave driver (supervisor). Those who rely on a supervisor to push them are usually low engine workers. Your engine can have an impact on promotions, salary, bonus, and general morale towards you in the working unit so, this is typically where high engine workers excel.

This engine concept is valid to some extent, but I don't believe it should be applied to people using God's gift as a hobby or to make a living. If you are using the Most High's gift and you try to apply this concept in hopes of increasing profit, production, or some other worldly gain, you may fail utterly. You may begin forcing your gift in ways and areas that it is not intended to be used. This can lead to small failures, and may even cause one to think that they are losing their gift or to doubt their gift. Under this concept, their gift is simply being misused or used untimely. There is a time and place for everything. Western society has the idea of more is better and that is the basic idea behind the engine concept, but the Bible's concept of what is enough or needed is different.

Western culture typically leans toward filling demand until the market is oversaturated and then it lets price and supply correct itself for demand, but in life, the Most High gives you what you need when you need it. This also applies to your gifts. Sometimes there's a surplus left, but most of the time, it's just enough.

> *Acts 2:43-46*
> *43 And fear came upon every soul: and many wonders and signs were done by the apostles.*
> *44 And all that believed were together, and had all things common;*
> **45 And sold their possessions and goods, and parted them to all men, as every man had need.**
> *46 And they, continuing daily with one accord in the temple, and breaking bread from house to house, did eat their meat* **with gladness and singleness of heart,**

PERSONAL REFLECTION

If you are using your gift and running into what feels like a wall or a dead end, sometimes you need to stop and check back in with your motives and heart (the heart; where you receive the voice of the Holy Spirit) to make sure that you are still on the right road. One can become so entangled with their gift that they forget about the overall path of the strait and narrow and the journey to the Kingdom. Be sure that you're serving the Most High and not your gifts.

None of this is in absolutes, meaning that I can only speak for myself. If I have learned anything about the Most High, it is that He uses principles and not rules. If everything was locked into rules, there would be no room for faith. The rules and the laws of physics show that men can't walk on water or move mountains with their mind. I say these things to say that there are always exceptions to the rule. Gifts vs. abilities is a concept that I typically encounter. I have seen people that blur or defy this concept but not many. This is just advice for someone trying to figure out their journey. Use this advice/concept until you get your own foothold and make your own concepts and understandings about gifts, ability, and even the Most High God. I struggle, even now, to convey what I perceive and understand with words. We just have to move forward on our journey and understanding will be given.

I believe we may subconsciously like grief because we don't take the work that the Most High gives us seriously. I believe the reason that we don't take our gifts seriously is because they aren't grievous for us to do. Without grief we don't feel like we are doing anything. That is slave conditioning. Regardless of how easy it is, continue to work until completion and enjoy the gifts and the rewards of your journey.

> Instruction: Don't try to apply the world's concept of hard work and reward to the Father's gifts because it can lead to unnecessary grief, misuse, a distorted negative view of your gift, and vanity. This is why it is important to recognize a gift versus an ability. You can continue to work hard on abilities but don't over stress your gifts. Let the Most High and synergy (discussed further later) do the heavy lifting. Your gifts don't work correctly under stress and force because this gift is the Spirit working in you; it's not you working within yourself, so why stress.

15
SYNERGY

Directly after Christ was baptized, he put a team together. In the Bible, Christ was almost never alone, yet most of us attempt and are content to use our gifts for the Father alone. The structure of the New Testament itself requires synergy. Synergy is the cooperation of two or more participants, substances, or other agents to produce a combined effect greater than the sum of their separate effects. There was synergy between Christ and the apostles because the apostles and scribes recorded their own version of the events. The effects of Christ's life were greatly increased through synergy.

The Messiah wasn't recording himself. Third person accounts were used because anyone can make up hard to believe miraculous stories of themselves. Christ didn't tell you about the events in his life himself. Others told you the story of Christ. The New Testament is written from the perspective of the witnesses.

Synergy is when a group of people come together for the Most High to work in unity using their gifts to reconnect, build and further the Kingdom. Individuals working for the

Most High alone in their own manner are the fishermen that are moving toward the Kingdom that you will meet on the path of the strait and narrow. The power of synergy is a group of people working together to build something miraculous with non-grievous mindsets. During this time, everyone is giving and working together happily because our gifts are what we find pleasure in. When in synergy, your gift will be near its full potential.

> *1 Corinthians 12:4-7*
> *4Now there are **diversities of gifts**, but **the same Spirit**.*
> *5And there are **differences of administrations**, but **the same Lord**.*
> *6And there are **diversities of operations**, but it is **the same God which worketh all in all**.*
> *7But the **manifestation of the Spirit is given to every man to profit** withal.*

The Most High is in full motion and at full effect on the Earth when He can fully operate through His people in collaboration while they're doing exactly what He created and designed them to do. This outcome always beats human expectations. It should be noted that, the process of synergy is done in a completely willing fashion, while rejoicing and praising the Most High, because everyone involved knows and understands that this is only possible through the Father and that He will receive all the glory, honor and credit. All activity is non-grievous and no one feels like they are being forced or receiving unfair wages.

Participants should understand that the greatest compensation and reward comes from the Most High. Not being paid well enough is not a barrier. Every worker is worth his wages. With that being said, that doesn't mean that there won't be sacrifices. Willful sacrifice is not grievous, in the same way that fasting with a purpose isn't starving. This is also why your gift is that thing that you will do for free. Profit should be equitably distributed, but part of your compensation is just the ability to perform for the Most High.

> *1 Timothy 5:18*
> *18 For the scripture saith,* **thou shalt not muzzle the ox** *that treadeth out the corn. And, The* **labourer is worthy of his reward***.*

When the term synergy alone is used, I'm typically not referring to family. A man and his family are one; that is a type of synergy. But the next level of synergy comes from multiple men and multiple families working together.

INDIVIDUALITY

Our current lack of synergy is a result of scattering. We were scattered physically, but we were also scattered mentally. Our mindsets are divided by the guise of individuality. We want to be so different and individual that it is hard for us to work together. Everybody thinks that they have the best idea, but greater than the best idea individually is working on an okay idea together.

The spreading out of the gifts to the four corners of the earth is the lessening of our synergy. The Most High knew that together is where our strength comes from, so the only way to punish us was to spread us out. Bringing these families back together is the start of the synergy and the restarting of our true culture. Many of us don't know our heritage, so we don't know why we're inclined to do certain things.

KNOW THY FAMILY

If you are fortunate enough to start in a good space with your father or a mentor that has a craft, then you should. This craft is related to your father's gift. He will have insights that only the gifted can see. He will be able to pass these insights on to you, and what would normally be an ability for you could be translated into a gift. Sometimes the difference between a gift and an ability is just knowledge and understanding concerning a skill. If a gifted person has enough understanding to make you see and understand their gift in the same light or manner that they see the craft in, I would venture to say that you were passed a gift.

If they can perfectly translate their insights to you through the spirit, you're primed for a new gift, Most High willing. For example, if I could give you the same body and understanding that Wembanyama has, you may be ready to step into the league. If I could perfectly transfer Maya Angelou's experiences, education, and understanding to you, you may become a generational poet. This is the opportunity a father has with a son. It's the opportunity to pass on experience, knowledge, understanding, and correction. An earthly father has the opportunity to correct and lead you the same way the heavenly Father corrects and leads us through the Holy Spirit.

> Proverbs 1:8-9
> *8My son, hear the instruction of thy father, and*
>   *forsake not the law of thy mother:*
> *9For they shall be an ornament of grace unto thy*
>   *head, and chains about thy neck.*

Many of these gifts that we have are passed down through our lineages. You often see that children of good singers tend to be good singers. That may be a taught craft or a natural gift. Either way, it's passed down. The underlying gift of singing could be an ear to hear notes and identify them or it could be to mimic the sounds you hear. If the father is a good athlete, many times the son will be a good athlete. Teaching at an early age can influence one's body and turn on certain genetic markers. Teaching at an early age can also influence one's mind and brain development in the same way. This is seen in the Bible where certain tribes had certain gifts and duties.

Crafts were passed down through the lineages, but because we are scattered most don't even know what the gifts of their grandparents and great grandparents were; much less the familial craft secrets. We don't know where our gifts are coming from, but they are coming from somewhere. I'm a natural at certain things and when I talk to my grandmother, she'll say, "well, your grandfather was good at that," or "your great uncle was good at that." Because these things aren't recorded and available to me, I was under the assumption that I'm different and I'm just good at certain things, but come to find out, there are other people in the family that have the same inclinations.

Don't forsake the craft of your father. Even if you later find out that your gift is something else entirely or unrelated to your father's craft, learning and mastering his or the family's craft doesn't hurt. While learning the craft, you are increasing the empire of your Father and family name in the same way that Jacob increased his father-in-law, Laban. This continuation of the family's craft reduces more scattering. You picking up where your forefather left off is progressional synergy. You are able to improve your father's processes and bounce ideas off of him and others to increase the knowledge of the craft for the entire family to use.

As a people, our strength comes from togetherness, so a

unique craft tailored to you isn't as important as the progressional synergy created from learning your father's craft. You have to consider the true simplicity of your gift and how it ties in with your family. If you are a healer, consider what makes you a good healer. What is the root?

Even if you have a different plan for your gift, the root of your gift will most likely tie into the family craft in one way or another. Why start from scratch if you can start from where your father left off? Why start a unique craft and discover new trade secrets on your own when you can use your father's trade secrets and craft secrets? The craft of your father that I am referring to is not his gift but what he applies his gift to.

Our Father's gift is creation. We all have one Father and He is a Creator. There's a little bit of Him in all His children in the same way that there's a little bit of your mother and father in all your siblings. This is what relates us. A man and a woman come together to create life. If all the nation can come together in synergy to meet the bridegroom, which is Christ, we can create the next level of life, which is the Kingdom on Earth.

> Instruction: Take time to reflect on the opportunities for synergy that you let escape in your life. Now, use that reflection to identify what opportunities you are currently ignoring. Who are the people that will help you increase your gift and what are the barriers for working with them? Reach out to current potentials and stay aware of new potentialities.

16
ON POINT

In order to have your mind on multiple initiatives at once for the Most High, a team is required. Until you can acquire a team, keep your eye single. The completion pace with singular vision is definitely slower alone than with a team, and a single person taking on multiple initiatives is even slower. Almost nothing will end up being completed in a timely manner. The missed parts of order are often time and sequence. Multiple tasks or efforts give/add more than a man can handle alone. Even when adding a group of people to help, the actual managing of people can become an additional task that is too much to bear. So when dealing with a group, seek a group leader whose talent is managing people.

The scriptures say to keep your eye single and it also says that the Most High will never give you more than you can bear. That is because the Most High made us to only be able to bear the singleness of eye. Without a team, there are just too many solutions to think of at once for one person. We can barely bear the complexity of just one of the Most High's solutions therefore, keep it simple.

Hearing from the Spirit is a very consuming task of listening. When you hear from the Spirit, what time is given for you to start the task? Is it 4:00 PM later today, tomorrow, or next year? The Spirit deals in the now, so when you get a single idea, the time to start putting it into motion is now. "Now" means to at least start the detailed planning and to do whatever preparation is possible.

If you've ever heard from the Spirit, you know how elusive the Voice is, especially if you're not focused and listening for it. You really have to be paying attention. Now, think about hearing two sets of instructions for two different activities at once from the voice of the Spirit and randomly receiving hints and instructions on where to go and what to do next. Your perception of the Most High's voice would have to be next level to be able to decipher all of the details. Even in the Bible when the Word or Voice of God came saying instructions, there was only one plan given at a time.

Beware of conflicting thoughts and ideas when you are working in full stride on your assignment for the Most High. As a distraction, the adversary will bring more ideas to halt your progress by dividing your attention. Write those additional ideas down and if they are actually from the Spirit, return to them after the completion of what you're already working on. These ideas may be the next part of your plan, but if they are not crucial to moving forward, keeping your eye single at this time is how to keep the main thing the main thing.

FOCUS POINT

If our eye is single and focused on what is in front of us, how do we find time for other things in our life? Your eyes can only focus on one plane of sight at a time. If you hold your finger up directly in front of you and focus on it, the objects behind your finger will be blurry or out of focus. Your finger, at this point, is currently the foreground and the focus of your central vision, and you can see all the details of your finger. If you focus on the objects in the background behind your finger, the background will come into focus and your finger will appear to have doubled/blurred. While focused on the background, you can see what appears to be two images of your finger and no details of the finger are perceptible. The mind works in this same manner.

When you focus on things in the background, the challenge/weight of the task in the foreground will appear to have doubled. It is also near impossible to focus on two unrelated thoughts at once. One thought will be in the foreground and the other thought(s) will be in the background. Fighting to keep your focus where you want it is the battle. If you can control your focus point at all times, you will overcome all and have complete dominion. Your mind's eye should be focused on the central vision or task from the Most High as much as possible.

PERIPHERY LIFE

While looking at your finger, you can also see things to your far left and right. The far corners of your vision are called peripheral vision. When objects come into your peripheral vision, if deemed necessary, your attention goes to that object and that brings the object into your central vision. Skilled performers and athletes can address things in their peripheral vision without taking their eye off of the goal or the ball. Using their peripheral vision while staying on task is fundamental to their success.

Generally, you will first listen to the voice of the Spirit and act on periphery tasks as they come. Peripheral tasks can be just as important as main tasks because in order for you to proceed, they still need to be completed. You will find that a key characteristic of many peripheral tasks is that they can be easily handled by hiring someone else to do them. The question that you want to ask yourself is, "Can this be done by someone else and result in the same outcome as when I do it?" If so, there is a high chance that it is peripheral.

Many times, you will find that what is central to you is peripheral to others and what is peripheral to others is central to you. This is how synergy was designed by the Most High. The Kingdom was, is, and will be built on interlocking building blocks. We are those building blocks.

> *1 Peter 2:4-6*
> *4 To **whom coming**, as unto **a living stone**, disallowed indeed of men, but chosen of God, and precious,*
> *5 **Ye also, as lively stones**, are built up a spiritual house, an holy priesthood, **to offer up spiritual sacrifices**, acceptable to God by <u>the Son of God</u>, Christ.*
> *6 Wherefore also it is contained in the scripture, **Behold, I lay in Sion a chief corner stone**, elect, precious: and he that believeth on him shall not be confounded.*

Christ is the cornerstone on which everything is built. We are the interlocking bricks, and the golden rule is the mortar. The golden rule is what binds and keeps us together as the structure becomes more complex.

> *Matthew 22:37-40*
> *37 <u>The Son of God</u> said unto him, Thou shalt **love the Lord thy God with all thy heart, and with all thy soul, and with all thy mind**.*
> *38 This is the first and great commandment.*

> *39 And the second is like unto it, Thou shalt **love thy neighbour as thyself**.*
> *40 On these **two commandments hang all the law and the prophets**.*

AS THE KINGDOM IS BUILT, the complexity of the structure will inevitably create opportunities for gaps in thought and perspective. Thus, the only thing that can hold us together is our love toward one another. When there is an opportunity to manipulate the Word and take advantage of others, we must not. We should defer to the love of the brotherhood. Unjustness, whether it is real or only perceived, must be quashed not only by authority but by the perceived doer of unjustness. Unjustness should be resolved before reaching a judge. That means there must be grace and mercy on both parts, the plaintiff and the defendant.

Instruction: The focus is to build singleness. First, allow peripheral tasks to be handled by someone else as their central task. This creates clear visions by removing distraction and clutter. Second, operate in the love of the brotherhood with grace and mercy. This removes peripheral clutter from the larger body (nation) as a whole. In this, the vision of the nation of Christ will be single.

17
FISHERMEN CERTIFICATION LEVELS

It is important to track your spiritual progress because awareness is key to growing. Taking a tally of the areas that you are strong and weak in can help you make better decisions in critical moments. Let's explain and address the levels that a fisherman progresses through first and then discuss their importance. These levels are for your personal records and should not be flaunted. This is an intrapersonal progression.

> *Ephesians 6:10-12*
> 10 Finally, my brethren, **be strong in the Lord**, and **in the power of his might**.
> 11 **Put on the whole armour of God**, that ye may be able to stand against the wiles of the devil.
> 12 For we wrestle not against flesh and blood, but against principalities, against powers, against the rulers of the darkness of this world, against spiritual wickedness in high places.

GARRETT JACKSON

ARMOR LEVELS

Armor Level 1 - Inner Confrontation

Your armor level is the measure of your overall ability to resist the darkness inside of you and in the world. Inner confrontation is the spiritual battle that happens within the heart. When you are in a room alone at night and the adversary or your flesh approaches, there is a confrontation. Someone who is at armor level 1 has the ability to win this internal fight but will still willingly approach the battle without being forced even though the voice of the Spirit says not to. As an example, if you are in a room alone and your flesh is desiring bacon, you will potentially get up and put yourself in the presence of bacon because your flesh desires it. This is the starting point of your fight for level 1.

At this level, sometimes you will win the fight and sometimes you will succumb to your desires. This is based upon your level of observation (discussed in the next section of this chapter). The willpower to overcome this type of confrontation comes from your spirit and can be strengthened through the Holy Spirit using prayer and desire. Willpower (choice) comes from your muscle of self control.

Armor Level 2 - Inner Avoidance

Armor level 2 is very similar to armor level 1 except when alone and tempted by the flesh or the adversary, you will never move towards a confrontation willingly. You have the ability to resist the voice of the adversary telling you to approach something that you should not and to obey the voice of the Comforter telling you to be still. At this level, when the flesh desires pork, you will never move to observe bacon by choice. You will not let bacon enter into your mind's eye. Because you have totally avoided it, you won't fall prey to this test when alone.

Armor Level 3 - External Confrontation

At level 2, you can overcome inner confrontation by avoiding the presence of temptation, but what will you do when the confrontation is presented from an external source? Level 3 consists of those that have mastered the internal and are dealing with the temptation that originates outside of one's self, sometimes unexpectedly. An example of an external confrontation is when you have been doing good resisting internal desires and the advertising of pork, but then suddenly, your mother drops by with one of your favorite childhood dishes. It just so happens to contain pork and she is expecting you to at least try it because she made it for you. Somebody who has mastered this level can overcome this confrontation by just telling their mother no, but someone just entering this level may still give in to the pressure of eating the dish.

Armor Level 4 - External Avoidance

A fisherman at the level 4 armor level, has mastered the first three armor levels and is wise enough to completely avoid the presence of external confrontations. You will never succumb to an opportunity to sin that you have not allowed near you. At level 4, if you think that you may fall into a confrontation, you won't go. If you see that sin has the ability to get close to you, you remove yourself from the situation. You don't allow yourself near the presence of sin or even the appearance of the presence of sin.

Following the voice of the Spirit is where the wisdom of

avoidance originates. Your uprightness is more important than you trying to prove that you are strong. At this level, your mother wouldn't bring you a pork dish because you would have already made it known to her that you are avoiding pork at all costs and no longer eating it. If she respects you and your decisions, she will not present you with choices that you have already given her the answer to.

OBSERVATION LEVELS

Observation Level 1 - See the Issue

Every armor level has 4 sub-levels that are called observation levels. Your level of observation is how well you can see your situation and the situations of others around you regarding sin. There is a wide spectrum of sin and your level of observation applies to each sin individually. This means that you have an observation level for each sin category.

The first level of observation is simply being able to see an issue and recognize that correction is needed. Seeing the issue is synonymous with hearing and identifying your instruction from the voice of the Spirit regarding a matter that you are confronted with. With the help of the Spirit, you can actively identify what is hindering progress, analyze the problem and understand what to do to stop from being hindered.

Even though you can see what to do next, you have no power to stop what is happening when at this level. You can hear the voice of the Comforter telling you to do something, and you can also identify the voice of the flesh/adversary telling you to do the opposite, but that is where your ability ends. This is the equivalent of knowing that you have diabetes and that you should stop eating sweets, but you don't have the willpower to stop. This inability to stop eating sugar is directly derived from gluttony. You can hear the Spirit telling you to make a better decision, but for some reason, you have not made the next step of actively making the correct choice in these moments.

> *Proverbs 25:27-28*
> *27*It is **not good to eat much honey***: so* for men to *search their own glory* is not *glory*.
> *28***He that** hath **no rule over his own spirit** is like *a city* **that is *broken down***, and ***without walls***.

Observation Level 2 - Fight the Issue

At Level 2, you have all of the ability of level 1 plus you can fight back against the test of sin. You are now in a battle and no longer watching yourself helplessly be a captive to sin. Sometimes you win and sometimes you don't, but the more that you fight, the stronger you become. The bottom line is that there is still a fight to be had. Continuing with the sugar example from above, instead of eating the sweets you now have the willpower to decide to obey the voice of the Spirit telling you not to eat it.

Observation Level 3 - Complete Defiance

Level 3 is attaining the ability to completely defy the voice of the flesh or the adversary. You can clearly hear (observe) the Spirit say yes or no regarding a sin or an issue and have the willpower to obey by choice consistently. At this point, this sin is no longer an issue for you. In the case of a diabetic, this level of willpower allows them to deny sugar every time.

Observation Level 4 - Complete Control

At Level 4, not only can you deny the unlawful issue access to you, but you can also completely use the issue in any manner for the good of the Most High. Using the diabetic example, if you were tempted by cakes, you would purchase them but not for you to consume yourself. They would be offered to others around you as a gesture of charity or a conversation starter to win a soul over to the Most High. Sweets become a tool and not a stumbling block that could harm you. These levels of observation can apply to any sin or issue that you are dealing with.

MIND'S EYE SIGHT LEVEL

Eye Sight Level 1 - Intermittent Vision

Level 1 eye sight means that you have intermittent control over what you focus your mind's eye on. A fisherman at this level can keep his eye focused on his task for a time but can be distracted. The distraction focuses the eye on something that may not be beneficial or expedient to the purpose of the fisherman. This movement of the eye away from its focal point is unintentional.

Eye Sight Level 2 - 20/20 Vision

Level 2 is a significant jump in ability over level 1. A fisherman with this level of sight is extremely rare. They have the ability to keep their eye trained on what they believe the Most High wants them to be focused on without limit. Distractions can't affect their focus and they can see their focal point with extreme clarity.

Eye Sight Level 3 - Clairvoyant Vision

The clairvoyant level of eyesight allows the fisherman to have all of the abilities of level 1 and 2 plus they have the attribute of fruition. What they consistently hold in their mind's eye and heart according to the will of the Most High eventually comes to fruition. A type of clairvoyance will be conveyed to those around if what the fisherman sees and says comes to pass. This belief comes to pass by consistently following the instructions of the Comforter. One may even call these types of fishermen prophetic, and their rarity is close to generational. The reason they are not generational talent is because any fisherman can elect to jump to this level by willpower at any time. This election comes from complete obedience, dedication, and sacrifice to the Most High no matter what is going on.

Armor/Resistance Levels
1. Inner Confrontation
2. Inner Avoidance
3. External Confrontation
4. External Avoidance

Observation Levels (Armor Sub-levels)
1. See the Issue
2. Fight Against the Issue
3. Complete Defiance
4. Complete Control

Mind's Eye Sight Levels
1. Intermittent Vision
2. 20/20 Vision
3. Clairvoyant Vision

LEVEL INTERACTIONS EXPLAINED

When analyzing the levels, understand that as a fisherman, you're going to level up, then down, and then up higher than you were before you initially leveled down. This is the process that most will endure. Some will level up faster than others and it is actually possible to skip levels. If a fisherman is able to gain the observation sub-level of complete control at any armor level, they have the potential to automatically jump to armor level 4 from any other armor level. The higher the observation levels are in all areas, the greater the strength of connection to the Comforter.

> Instruction: You have an observation level for every sin that you deal with or encounter. As you master your resistance against one sin, the devil may and most likely will approach with a different angle and a different sin category for you to overcome. Complete your armor and gain complete control over every sin that arises. Never become comfortable in your sin. People who become comfortable in their sin will try to normalize it and make it a new category, lifestyle, or quality for people to ascribe to. Remain comfortable in the Comforter. Being comfortable in the Comforter is equal to being uncomfortable in the world because the Spirit rebukes the malevolent ways, things, and images of the world.

18

TEMPTATION IS THE TEST

On your beautiful journey, temptation will be encountered. The Hebrew word for temptation is נָסָה *nasah*. The form of the word *nasah* is reference H5254 in the Strong's Concordance. It means to try; to prove; to test. Have you been tried, proven, and tested? Have you been passing your tests with flying colors?

These tests are how you become certified as a fisherman. Have you reached the top fisherman certification level in all of the sins that you are facing? When you understand that temptation is only a test, you will look at temptation totally different. The English word temptation sounds like something that's hard to beat, but a test, sounds like something that you can pass.

A test or trial is any time that you have a choice between hearkening to what the flesh is desiring or to what the Spirit is instructing. How you do on these trials determines whether your spirit or your flesh gets stronger. These choices will constantly come up so you will have numerous opportunities to prove yourself daily by passing these tests. Temptation isn't a bad word. It's an opportunity for success and growth for you and the tempter. You will find that your show of discipline over temptation may even provide an opportunity to influence the tempter toward the Most High.

> *James 1:2-4*
> *2**My brethren, count it all joy when ye fall into divers temptations;***
> *3Knowing this, that the trying of your faith worketh patience.*
> *4But let patience have her perfect work, **that ye may be perfect and entire, wanting nothing.***

MANAGING YOUR ENCOUNTERS WITH TEMPTATION

You must determine your own course load. This means to take the test that you are forced to take but you can also avoid taking unnecessary tests by controlling your position. The avoidance of a test is a successful test score in and of itself. Oftentimes, we must distance ourselves from sin, so setting yourself apart is equivalent to avoiding tests.

Most tests will be by suggestion but sometimes they are unavoidable. In these instances, you still have the opportunity to make a decision in accordance with the Spirit. The Most High will always give you a choice. If He did not, the Most High wouldn't be allowing you to prove yourself. Free choice means that the Most High has given you the opportunity to deliver yourself; to Him or to the adversary. It is only when you fail to come to Him that He must intervene to deliver you, if and once you call upon Him.

TEMPTATION ON A FORK

You may now look at the devil differently. When you hear the phrase, "the devil comes to tempt you," it sounds like he's coming with all the earthly things that you already enjoy or desire like pastries, wine, cars, or money, and sometimes the devil does come with these things. It is not often, but when the devil does come with these things the test is much more advanced because it is an obvious exchange.

The difference between a sin of exchange and the basic type of sin is the immediacy of the gratification. For example, a guy might commit a crime to get money so that he can impress a girl with the spoils and potentially get her. This is basic temptation because there are still contingencies that may or may not come to pass. What the guy initially wanted was the girl. If this were an exchange temptation, the guy would have been propositioned to receive the girl in exchange for the crime. Thus, getting what he initially wanted as soon as the act was completed.

> Matthew 4:1,8-9
> *1Then was* <u>the Son of God</u> ***led up of the Spirit into the wilderness to be tempted of the devil****.*
> *8Again, the devil taketh him up into an exceeding high mountain,* ***and sheweth him*** *all the kingdoms of the world, and* ***the glory of them****;*
> *9And saith unto him,* ***All these things will I give thee, if thou wilt fall down and worship me.***

Wanting a girl is not a bad thing. Wanting money or resources is not a bad thing. Fruitfulness through lineage and your storehouse are actually things that are promised by the

Most High if you follow Him. The things promised are not the sin, but what the devil wanted in exchange for the things already promised is the sin.

These temptations will consist of at least two options that are called forks in the road. No matter how hard the choice seems you will always have an option. The option most beneficial to your Spirit will draw you nearer to the Most High and the options most beneficial to your flesh will lead you further away from the Most High.

On your journey, forks will be presented over and over in different ways and at different times. How you choose over time represents the ways of your heart. Your choices throughout your journey of a fisherman informs the Most High who you truly are. These choices also confirm whether or not you are letting your flesh override the person that He knew you to be in the womb.

> *Jeremiah 17:10*
> *10I the LORD search the heart, I try the reins, even to give every man **according to his ways**, and **according to the fruit of his doings**.*

THE DEVIL CAN'T TRICK THE LIGHT

This word "temptation" sounds like you will be presented with a situation that involves being tricked. That's not the case. You already know all the answers to the tests and pop quizzes if you are a son of the Most High. The answers are provided by the Comforter in every test you will ever endure. She is our cheat sheet.

What if I were to tell you that the devil is coming to give you a test, and that every day you will get quizzed. If you pass the test and quizzes, you will get eternal life. This would sound like a challenge that is worth taking versus it sounding like the devil being this all-powerful evil being that is coming to send you to hell. The devil is more like a proctor that is coming to give you a test.

A proctor doesn't create the answers to the test. They don't grade the tests. They don't even determine who can take the tests. A proctor purely administers (gives) the test, monitors the test, and collects the results. This is closer to the actual role of the devil than what our culture portrays it to be. Your actions determine your answers to the questions, and then, the Most High determines between Heaven and hell when He grades your test at the judgement. If you don't know the answers to your test, choose the answer that puts the Most High first.

This is the concept of understanding temptation and understanding the priority that should be given to the Most High. When the voice of the adversary calls to you in the same way it called to Christ on the mountain, know that it is only a test. Know that the success of the Most High is already written. You are already written of.

TESTS WHILE IN SYNERGY

While in synergy, the voice of the Comforter is paramount because of the corruption of man. It is hard to see where corruption is coming in, especially when there are many angles and people involved in a matter. The adversary and his organizations attack at a personal level to hurt a group. They target individuals and seek to gain leverage over them. Know and understand that these individuals will be sent, either by their internal motivations or outside leveraged coercion.

This process is the internal war of growth. Attempts of infiltration into the kingdom on Earth are inevitable. Your climbing of fisher certification levels, indicates that you trust your connection to the Comforter beyond what others tell you due to potential corruption and rebellion. Two or more in the Spirit in agreement is a sign of the Comforter. One man alone or singled out can lead you astray, so when there is something in question or doubt, two or more fishermen should agree on the matter; the more senior, the better. This is what keeps corruption, personal agendas, and adversarial agendas at bay.

> *Luke 22:28-29*
> *28 Ye are they which have continued with me in my temptations.*
> *29 And I appoint unto you a kingdom, as my Father hath appointed unto me;*

There is no need to panic or worry. The adversary can't prevail over the Most High as long as you make sure that your fisherman level is higher than the level of the deus deceptor sent by the deceiver. The deceptor knows all darkness but is blinded by the light. Righteousness, godliness, faith, love patience, meekness, and thanksgiving blinds the deceiver, so follow the light of the Comforter.

> Instruction: What is your test? What are the forks that you're dealing with right now? If you haven't understood what you're dealing with, know that even if you continue reading, you won't truly move on until you have grasped and mastered this concept.

19
FIND PEACE BEFORE THE FURNACE

Isaiah 48:9-11

9 For my name's sake will I defer mine anger, and for my praise will I refrain for thee, that I cut thee not off.

10 Behold, **I have refined thee**, but not with silver; **I have chosen thee in the furnace of affliction.**

11 For mine own sake, even for mine own sake, will I do it: for how should my name be polluted? and **I will not give my glory unto another**.

The Most High has preserved a remnant of His people to keep His name alive. Our only purpose is to serve Him. Serving Him means to follow the four pillars of the fisherman and to walk in his ways following the Holy Spirit. This is the example that Christ left for us and what the Most High's children are put here to do. We know that every one of His people aren't up to the call, so the Most High is filtering and refining us like silver and gold. Fishermen who are called but not chosen will be shown through this refinement process. Those who are not pure will be purified by the Most High, not man.

The furnace of affliction is the flesh. Our bodies generate the heat/pressure that turns our spirits and souls into gold. When you are in long suffering or undergoing a test, you will feel this pressure. This pressure is what defines us. Will we remain as the dust of the earth or will we be redefined as a precious metal from the Earth, such as silver or gold?

> Zechariah 13:9
> 9 And I will bring the third part **through the fire, and will refine them as silver is refined, and will try them as gold is tried: they shall call on my name, and I will hear them:** I will say, It is my people: and they shall say, The LORD is my God

Even as a child, there were situations in which we felt pressured by those around us. Notice what the body does when under pressure; it heats up. When you were young and with your family, they would put you on the spot and tell you to dance. They would say it's your turn and would chant "Go (insert your name here) Go (insert your name here), it's your birthday." They expected you to dance at the drop of a dime. If you were shy, not that good of a dancer, or just didn't want to entertain, your body would become warm because of the pressure.

Think back to when you were with a group of your friends. The group was plotting on doing something nefarious but internally, something (the Holy Spirit) was telling you that it's not the right thing to do. There was a pressure to participate because everyone else was doing it. At this time, your body began to heat up. You were forced to decide one way or another.

When you were in class and the teacher told you to stand up and read or present your project, your body began to heat up. Your bowels may have felt weird as well. How you performed in that moment determined a portion of your grade in class. The more prepared you were for the situation, the less pressure you felt. This is the same with the Most High. The more that you have read the scriptures, meditated on His Word, and trusted in His voice, the less pressure you will feel. Your performance in class hinged on how much of your time you gave to preparing for the presentation.

Although these are just basic examples in life, tests from the Most High have the same consistency, and your body acts in the same exact way. Your performance in the class of life hinges on how much time you give to the Most High. This is your preparation. Time given to the Most High purifies the flesh, so there is less to burn off in the furnace of affliction in high pressure moments. You will notice that the more time you give to the Most High, the easier it is to overcome these tests. Devotion (proper preparation) is the antithesis of pressure.

Devotion to the Most High brings peace; including peace of mind. Peace is the opposite of tension, stress, and pressure. The more of the Most High that you have internalized, the more gold you have in your core and the less pressure that you will feel. This is because your priorities have already been decided. They have already began to become solidified. When you gave time and devotion to the Most High, you made a decision that He was more important than anything else at that time. These are the types of moments that define what you are made of.

Will you rise to the occasion or falter? Will you give your best effort? Will you try your best, fail, and then quit, or will you fail and use that failure as motivation to become better? Will your experience of failure make you so strong that that object of failure can never dominate you again? Will you have dominion over your life, or will your failures have dominion over you?

As you grow older, you will encounter more advanced and more complex high-pressure situations. They will usually include money, people of the opposite sex, relationships, and obedience to the values that you learned from your family. There is no one right answer for every situation, but the constant will always be the voice of the Comforter. This is the law that is written on your heart. The way to keep you tuned and aligned with the Most High is to fellowship with Him. Commune often with the scriptures. This will strengthen your resolve and make clear to you your paths.

The main characteristic of gold is its resilience and how it is unbothered by its environment. It doesn't tarnish when exposed to moisture and it is resistant to chemical reactions. When people are in high pressure situations, they sweat. Their bodies also produce chemical reactions in the brain and bowels. Will this moisture make you tarnish? Will you fold, or remain resistant to the bodily reactions? This is what determines if you are gold.

We are being tested daily to determine the substance of our make-up. On the earth, we walk on what we are made of, dirt (dust/carbon). In the kingdom of Heaven, we will also walk on what we are made of, gold. In Revelation, John speaks about streets that are paved with gold, and those of us who make it, will walk on them. The minimum that you must be is the lowest thing where you reside. The ground. Residents of the Kingdom must be made of gold. Let's become gold.

> *Revelation 21:21*
> 21 And the twelve gates were twelve pearls; every several gate was of one pearl: and the street of the city was pure gold, as it were transparent glass.

20
DECEPTOR

At the beginning of this book you were probably more familiar with the deus deceptor/evil genius than you were the Comforter/Holy Spirit. It's probably because we assume or are taught that the naughty voice inside of our heads is us and the positive voice is our conscience. We were taught wrong. Neither one of those voices are you. You are the thinker in the middle that makes the choice. You are the observer between the two that silences both voices by observing. The voice becomes silent so that they can hear what you are about to think or say mentally. You are the awareness that is trying to choose between the two. The scripture says to take no thought regarding what you are about to say because the presence of your thoughts disrupts the Spirit.

> *Matthew 10:19-20*
> *19But when they deliver you up, take no thought how or what ye shall speak: for it shall be given you in that same hour what ye shall speak.*

> *20For it is not ye that speak, but the Spirit of your Father which speaketh in you.*

    The Deus Deceptor is the darkness. This is what the Most High separated from the light, which is Christ, in the beginning. If Christ is the firstborn, I would venture to say that the deceiver is the second. The moment that light was created a shadow was created in the same exact shape. If Christ has the shape of man, so does the shadow. When you stand in the sun, your shadow is an exact outline of you except that it is distorted by whatever it is cast upon. This is why the deceiver is so cunning. It is because he can look like Christ. He can look like righteousness, but he is not.

    The plans that you receive to do evil come so quickly and seemingly complete. They seem readily executable and whenever you think of an obstacle, there is a quick answer for how to overcome it. They often offer a quick reward or payday. The goals of these plans are usually to acquire more for personal gain. Notice how genius and bulletproof you believe these evil plans are when they come to you. This false confidence is a hallmark of plans sent from the deceiver.

    When have you ever had that much confidence and faith in a righteous plan sent from the Holy Spirit? It is impossible to be for the Most High and against Him at the same time, so people usually don't steal, kill, and scam to give money to a church or to donate it. That's usually only seen in movies and tv shows. The plans that come from the deceiver are only good enough to fool the flesh and your spirit, if your spirit is following after or chasing fleshly desires. These evil engineered plans cannot fool the Holy Spirit or your heart if you are a son of the Most High and a brother of Christ. If you are a child of the Most High and still become influenced by the deceiver, you were not fooled, you made a decision.

    Thus, it is upon the fishermen to let the children of the

Most High that are still in their ignorance, know that they are children of the Most High. This is the only way that they can stop being fooled by the deceptor and make a conscious choice to either follow the Most High or the deceptor. Until they have been presented with this choice, which is the choice of Christ, there is still an innocence within them. This is why we are told to go to the four corners of the Earth preaching the gospel of Christ.

The choice isn't a confession of their mouth but a path of their lives. Confessing the kingdom of Christ with your mouth but not building it with your actions nullifies your confession. If you choose the deceptor at any point, you are acting as an agent of the deceptor. The same sins that the deceptor uses to destroy us, the Most High uses as an opportunity to refine us.

ENTERTAINMENT

Entertainment is the antithesis of work(s) and the tool used for mass destruction by the deceptor. It is dangerous to your fruitfulness and ethic because it is still-inducing. A hallmark feature of entertainment or being entertained is no physical movement or motion of the body. The only visibly active body part while being entertained is the eye and rarely the hands. Watching a game is entertainment. Playing a game is not. Participation alters entertainment and turns it into some form of work. The people watching the basketball game paid to see it. The people playing in the basketball game are being paid to play. This form of work could be paid but it could also just be an exercise or workout. In this case, physical or mental health is the reward. Either way, there is only a benefit to the worker. Therefore, entertainment must be limited or your greatest resource will be squandered. Outside of sleeping, entertainment is the quickest and easiest way to spend what resource you have so little of, time.

The person watching a movie is being entertained but the actors, directors and people on the set are working. What are they working towards? Expressing an idea through a story much like the Messiah expressed concepts through parables. Being entertained is eerily close to being taught. That's because you are being taught when you're being entertained.

The appearance and posture of someone being taught is often identical with someone being entertained. The only difference with a tv show is that you are on your couch and not in a classroom. Yes, you are more comfortable on your couch and you can relax and slouch, but think back to your classrooms when you were a child. Recall all of the times that your teachers asked you or your classmates to sit up straight. After a certain amount of time in this state of receiving with your eyes and ears, the rest of your body begins to lose its posture. It's because your body is dormant during this process. It's not doing any work.

Receiving and learning is good up to a certain point, but what is learned eventually needs to be practiced and improved upon. In the classroom, we were supposed to be learning things that would be helpful in life. We were taught the same subjects day after day at the same time of the day. We were being programmed. To be taught means to be programmed. Being programmed isn't necessarily a bad thing. Your parents programmed behaviors into you by the things that they told you and showed you. Think about the behaviors the tv shows are teaching us through their programming.

The main program being shown on television is fear. Fear is anti-bravery, anti-faith and anti-hope. Fear is only helpful when it is preventing you from doing evil. It is not helpful when it stops you from doing the right thing. Programming someone is easier than you might believe. If a woman watches a show where innocent women are being kidnapped while walking down the street, this will implant a seed of fear. This can cause women to walk down the street by themselves less, not because it is dangerous, but because she now believes the chance of getting kidnapped is higher.

In shows, sometimes the criminal is caught before harm is done but sometimes the criminal is not caught at all. Going on walks is healthy. Jogging is healthy. Now, a form of doubt is put into a woman's mind that it is healthy to do these things but unsafe. This concept of fear is in direct contrast to the theme, "the wicked will be punished and the righteous will be covered" that the Bible portrays. If women never saw tv shows like this, would their activity be different? If the Most High needs this woman to walk down the street, will she?

According to the Bible, the wicked should be afraid and the righteous should be courageous. You will need courage to move on the instructions of the Comforter. Entertainment can inhibit this movement and in many cases, programs you to lean away from the orders of the Most High.

> Instruction: Seek the voice of your Father. Daily, wake up and decide who your father will be. Make a conscious and noted choice. With a complete control observation level, think about what you could do with the situation presented. Who could be delivered? — Fear God. We must deprogram ourselves from the world's programming and reprogram ourselves with the program of the Spirit and the laws written. Our hope is to find the programming of the Holy Spirit. This starts with reading, receiving, and listening to the Word.

21

BE THE PROCESS

The scientific method involves observing while carefully questioning what you see in your observation. This observation and questioning will bring you to a conclusion, which will become your hypothesis. This hypothesis must be tested to see if what you thought you observed is true. If what you observed is true, the circumstances can be repeated, and as long as all conditions are met, you should come to the same conclusion of your hypothesis. If your hypothesis turns out to not be true, you must re-evaluate your observation to figure out what you truly observed and why you can't repeat it. Then you test your new hypothesis. This is a summary of the scientific method.

We must use this same method with the Most High. Why? Because He uses it on us. He tries us to see what we are made of. He tries us to see if we are His children. He chastises us to see if we will come to Him or turn towards evil once our toughened stiff-necked exterior has been broken. Thus, we must try the Most High to see if He is true. In Psalm 34, David speaks of the scientific method. Verse 6 is

David's observation. Verse 7 is his hypothesis. Verse 8 is his concluded theory/law.

> *Psalm 34:6-8*
> *6 This **poor man cried**, and the **LORD heard him**, and saved him out of all his troubles.*
> *7 The **angel** of the LORD **encampeth** round about **them that fear him**, and **delivereth them**.*
> *8 **O taste and see that the LORD is good**: **blessed is the man that trusteth in him**.*

The conclusion/theory/law is that those who trust in the Most High will be blessed. If you know Him, you know that He is good. If you don't know Him, try Him. If you don't believe the process that I am describing in this book, try it fully and correctly. If it fails, examine your ways and consult your Word. If you still don't believe, I urge you to look for your own process while watching for chastisement to gauge your actions and the results of them correctly.

If you go deep enough into science you'll eventually get to the spiritual. Going deep into quantum mechanics will lead you to the spiritual world or as some would call it, the world of expectation and hope. In quantum physics, you will see how your observations, thoughts, and expectations (hope) affect the way that particles in their lowest forms move, perform, and behave. Particles, such as photons (light particles), are affected by merely observing or gauging them. This is called the observer's effect. This means that massless particles such as photons move as expected by the observer. The particles can't be observed in their natural state because your belief/expectation of how they will move or perform is how they will move and perform. This has been proven through the double-slit experiment.

Something else also can't behave naturally under observation and is massless. It's your thoughts. When under the observation of your attention and the glare of your mind's eye, your thoughts and their patterns will be affected. When you observe your thoughts consciously, they stop and behave how you expect until you lose focus or attention. Then they return back to operating as if they are out of your gaze. I propose that this is because photons and thoughts operate on the same plane of existence. They are both massless particles of light/electricity. The only difference is that one of them is perceived to be in your body and the other is perceived to be outside of it.

If photons have the ability to pass through solid objects, I theorize that thoughts do too. This is becoming more and more apparent with the new neural science that scientists and Tesla are testing. These electrical neural pulses, that are our thoughts, that Tesla is able to perceive and transform into mechanical actions and digital intentions are the proof. I also believe that this tech is dangerous because just as photons can be influenced by an observer so can your thoughts which are photon adjacent. This is a topic for another book so I won't keep going, but please know that the science will always lead you back to the spiritual and vice versa. It is upon the fishermen, with the understanding of this type of advanced knowledge, to remain aware and vigilant, and to raise a warning flag when the time comes.

> Instruction: Your first science project in life should be proving the Most High. There will be a spiritual knowing that is confirmed when there are so many coincidences observed that they start to add up to certainty.

22
WITHOUT A LIST YOU'RE LISTLESS

Fishermen will be tried and proven many times, and they must try and prove the things around them many times. When you build a structure, you initially prove the structure to make sure that it is sturdy enough to handle the load that you intend to place on it. You will find that testing or inspecting it again is periodically needed to make sure that a structure like a bridge, highway, or a home isn't failing. It is the same for building the Kingdom. What the Kingdom is comprised of must be tested and tested again. Your inner-man is the first structure that you will build with these techniques, and your processes of proving should be recorded and written down.

Included in your process of proving is a list of the things that the Most High has asked you to do. The things that He has asked you to do are derived from the things that you have asked of Him. The list must be recorded in order of importance. Chronological order is the main factor that determines importance because time is the most crucial. No man knoweth of that day and hour not even the angels of heaven.

In terms of physical actions, your list is second only to

prayer. Write down the things that you believe the Spirit is telling you to do. Tasks from the Father, even the smallest, are important. If you forget a task or idea, it may not come back to you, or you may miss your opportunity to complete it.

Imagine Abraham forgetting that he was told to sacrifice Isaac. It sounds preposterous right? We forget to do things that the Father tells us to do all the time. Either we didn't know that He was the one that told us to do it, or we acknowledged that this may be an idea from the Spirit, but we were so overcome with life that it slipped our minds. We think and act like we are not as special as the figures in the Bible. For as long as we have been on this Earth, we act as though the Father has never wanted or asked us to do anything. If you haven't been acting like that, what has the Father ever asked you to do, and have you done it? No? The way we are currently operating, listless, says that we also think that the Father will never ask us to do anything.

<u>Listless</u>
- Having no desire or inclination; indifferent; heedless; spiritless.

Have there ever been parents that are in their children's lives that have never asked their children to do anything? Something as simple as being told to be quiet during certain times is still a request. It could also be something as simple as speaking up at certain times. As simple as the tasks of being quiet and speaking are, we can find them very difficult to do for the Father, especially in pressurized moments.

In Chapter 10, we spoke about being exact in what you order from the Most High. The list I'm speaking of in this chapter, is derived from that order. Recall the definition of a list.

List
- a number of connected items or names written or printed consecutively, typically one below the other.

The number of connected items are the steps you envisioned to complete your task. The order means nothing without action from you. The sole purpose of this list is a real-world reminder of what you're working on so that your eye is single and not distracted by mammon. In the beginning, it was spoken, but it was also written. How do we know it was written? Because in the beginning was the Word. It was not only heard, but it was also separated. This separation of the light is the establishing of order. This is equivalent to the Most High cleaning His room.

In this list, separate your central tasks from your peripheral tasks. Separate your original desires from the adjustments that the Most High has made when He directed your steps towards things not only desirable but beneficial. Consult the Most High daily regarding what it is that you have set out to do that coincides with your list.

The more inconsistent you are with your task list, the more inconsistent your life will be. Inconsistencies mean that your eye is not single towards the Most High and the purpose He has given you. Inevitably, there will be inconsistencies because of the weakness of the flesh, but you must remember that the kingdom of Heaven is at hand. This list is second only to prayer because it's not your list, it's God's list. Have you created your list yet?

Many times in the past, I've written a list of things that I believed I needed to accomplish for the Father, but some things didn't get done when I had the opportunity to do them. Some things didn't get done because they were too great to accomplish in a day, and some things didn't get done because of disorganization. I wasn't fully aware of how important the ideas coming to me were and that I needed a plan to get them accomplished. Note, there is a difference between writing something on your list with the intention of doing it and writing something on your list with a plan to do it.

<u>Definite</u>
- clearly stated or decided; not vague or doubtful.

The three major differences between "a things to do list" and a plan are time, detail (research), and definiteness. A things to do list is a list of things that you intend to do in no particular order. You can rank the items by what's most important to you, by what you want to do first, or by a variety of factors, but ultimately, it's still just a list of reminders.

If you want to go on vacation to a tropical island, at what point does this vacation go from an objective on your things to do list to something planned? It is when you introduce the variable of time. You don't have a plan without the variable of time. Your plan begins when you add a date to the objective. Now, you know how much time you have to prepare before the execution of the objective. After you pick a month and a day, you can look at plane tickets and cruise schedules to decide what is the best way to get to the island. Every plan begins with preparation.

Preparation includes gathering information and detail.

Even while dealing with a things to do list and turning objectives into plans, we should still be listening for the Comforter. The Spirit knows the way. We receive the objectives on the to do list, the plan, and the details to the plan from the Spirit.

Luke 14:28-30
28For which of you, **intending to build a tower, sitteth not down first, and counteth the cost**, *whether he have sufficient to finish it?*
*29***Lest haply, after he hath laid the foundation, and is not able to finish it***, all that behold it begin to mock him,*
30Saying, **This man began to build***, and was not able to finish.*

    The Spirit can bring you any type of details that you can imagine. In my experience, the Spirit brings me the details to the plan that are essential. The details that don't matter, the Spirit leaves to my desires. For example, if the Spirit said to rent a car and go to another state, the type of car may be given because that detail could matter. If in the next state, I need to pick up or haul something, that means I need something that can carry a payload. If I'm working on a tight budget and the distance is great, the Spirit may tell me to get a small car because it is better on gas. What the Spirit doesn't usually tell me is what color the interior should be. Should I pick a white car or a black car? The things that don't affect the mission aren't usually given. The things that don't matter are a part of the indefiniteness of the plan. The definiteness comes when you actually purchase the plane ticket or rental car. Now, you know exactly how much you've paid, and you can determine if you have to pay additional fees for luggage or additional money for gas. This is the definiteness of the plan. A well-defined plan accounts for everything. The more detail in the plan, the better, because that means that you're more prepared for the attacks of the adversary.

    The adversary is going to be there every single time you leave the house. The adversary's main goal is to slow you down with details. For example, if you leave the house with no toothbrush with the intention of buying one when you get to your destination, this provides an opportunity for the adversary to slow you down. You may get to your destination, and the nearest drug store may be out of toothbrushes, so now you have to drive 20 minutes further to get the toothbrush. This was not in your plan. Another example is, you plan to leave on Friday, and you have a list of things that you want to do before Friday, but you decide to leave two of those things to be done right before you leave. One of these things could be as simple as sending an email. You figured the email would take you 15 minutes to write up and you'll have an extra 30 minutes in your plan, but right before you hit send, the internet goes out. In this case, this email is vital to confirming the details of your plan and your internet was working fine for the entire week before. You could have easily sent the email and confirmed the details during that time. Now, you're stuck waiting for the internet to work, and your plan is time contingent. These are the types of instances the adversary uses to poke and prod.

> Instruction: The Most High only deals in the real so make lists based on your reality and your faith. Imagine a man watching a tv show or a video online and desiring and asking the Most High for the woman in the video to be his rib. This woman may not be available. She may not really be the person she's portraying herself to be. She may look totally different without make-up. The woman that this man is asking for doesn't exist as he perceives. It makes more sense for men to go out and meet women, and then ask the Most High for the real woman that they met. Imagine a person asking the Most High for a house based on a picture in the magazine. They don't know where the house is or how much

it costs. They don't know that this house had a bad foundation and burned down in the L.A. fires last year. How can the Most High deliver this house to them? It makes more sense to get a realtor to look at real houses and then ask the Most High for a plan to get the home that they desire. The Most High deals in the real so ask the Most High, and He will then provide instructions on how to pursue what you desire. You must then be aware enough to write down the instructions using the steps in this book.

23
LOOSE ENDS

Zechariah 13:4
4And it shall come to pass in that day, that *the prophets shall be ashamed every one of his vision, when he hath prophesied; neither shall they wear a rough garment to deceive:*

DREAMS AND EMOTIONS

Chapter 13 of Zechariah speaks of end-times before the last battle, and I believe it already has begun to come to pass. As you mature as a fisherman, your dreams will have more and more meaning. As the meaning increases, so will your understanding and interpretations of the dreams.

Dreams are not given to you to boast them over others but to give you gentle instruction and awareness of what's going on inside your heart. Dreams happen internally, and they should usually be kept to yourself or within a close trusted circle unless specifically told by the Comforter or the Word to share them publicly or to not seal them.

Dreams are another place where entertainment comes into play. Entertainment can cause us to imagine vain things, so you have to be careful to discern between which thoughts, visions, and dreams were planted by the deceiver through entertainment and those which come by the Comforter.

In terms of emotions, the mind can be just as real as life. Through night visions, the mind has the ability to produce all types of emotions and physical responses. Dreams can wake you up feeling angry, insecure, worried, or wanting revenge, but they can also be reassuring and make you happy or joyous. Tears from your eyes, sweat from your pores, a stress induced headache, and an increased heartbeat are all responses that can also be caused by dreams. This is the power of the mind.

Upon waking, you whole-heartedly feel emotions after certain dreams. What do you do with these emotions? Are they real and why are you feeling them? Emotional dreams are a way that the Most High uses to test the heart and how you truly feel about certain subjects. One thing that is tested during emotional night visions is your ability to forgive. If you wake up and hold on to the emotions evoked by your dreams all day, it is a sign that you have not mastered forgiveness or acquired the patience to deal with the type of situation that occurred in the dream.

Identify the emotion of the dream. Review the things that happened in the dream and seek to understand which detail in the dream caused you to feel this way. Examine the people involved, the material things, and the circumstance or event of the dream. Which one is causing the emotion?

An emotional dream will usually include protecting the people and the things that you care about the most. If you are still feeling a negative emotion from a dream, it is because there is a lack of trust in the Most High. When you can let go of all of these emotions and the things that are beyond your control, you have conquered the fear that causes the emotions.

Having complete dominion is the same as becoming a master. You don't have to worry about mastering the world; just master yourself and the world will follow. Part of mastering yourself is understanding emotion. A fisherman has one enduring emotion and many fleeting emotions. The six basic emotions are happiness, sadness, fear, disgust, anger, and surprise. They should all be used and manipulated in benefit of the Most High to further help the Most High's plan for you.

NUTRITION

Food and supplements are crucial for your journey. Your body requires these things and without them, you will become more susceptible to the temptation of comfort and wrath. You will be more likely to "turn" to other places for the typical chemicals that your brain supplies your body with through proper nutrition. These turns are usually addiction related activities, such as stimulants and sexual release. These addictions are only taking the place of the chemicals provided by the most natural addiction that the Most High has given you, food.

When you eat food, your body is releasing the same chemicals that stimulants and depressors release. All foods are drugs that heal, but certain foods like mushrooms, and opioid producing seeds have a stronger effect. Yes, food is required to live but so is the set of chemicals that is released with food. This is why when people are sad, stressed or unbalanced, they comfort eat.

A lack of proper nutrition will have you thinking that you are something that you are not. For instance, you may think that you are lazy, but what causes symptoms like sluggishness, low-energy, drowsiness, tiredness, depression, and fatigue? It could be a lack of one of the vitamins from the vitamin B complex. A lack of B12 can cause fatigue and weakness. A lack of B6 can cause depression and confusion. Vitamins B1 and B2 help convert food into energy, so without these, you could have low energy and reduced brain function. A lack of B3 and B9 can also cause fatigue. Someone who is missing these vitamins may confuse their physical state with their mental traits or personality. The entire time that you were thinking that you were consumed with laziness it was really malnourishment.

FASTING

Your influences, even nutritionally, should instruct or improve you morally and intellectually. The goal is for us to be in full control of our influences. The goal isn't to control the influencer in general but to control the influencer's access to us. If you're not in full control of the influence, then it is negative, and it will control you.

We must have discipline and restraint over the tools and aids that we use in life. We must be honest with ourselves and aware of ourselves enough to realize when something or someone is controlling our journey that doesn't edify us. The best way to control dependence and improve self-restraint is by fasting. Prayer and scripture are two things that are useful for keeping our minds occupied while fasting.

When we pray during fasting, it doesn't have to be the most complex prayer ever recited. Your mind and body will already be under stress because of the fast, so the simpler the prayers, the better. It is important that we keep a prayerful mind by keeping the Most High in the front of our minds. This is done simply by remembering Him throughout your day no matter what you're doing. When we starve ourselves without the mindset of fasting, emotions like anger (hangry) or sins that we comfort ourselves with have the opportunity to dominate us. If we are not specific in our intentions of hunger, these things can influence our moods without us knowing.

One fail-safe way to remember Him throughout the day while fasting is to say thank you to the Father. You can groan within yourself or under your breath. It doesn't have to be a loud thank you. This will keep a feeling of thanks towards the Most High that stimulates you and your body even in your time of lack.

We normally thank the Most High for the things that we have and our prosperity. Prosperity is the opposite of lack. A key to fasting is thanking the Most High when we are deprived or in lack. If you can thank the Most High through deprivation, it's sincere. This is practice for when you don't have all the things that you want. Even at times like this, the Father is still good. Try not to only thank Him with your mouth, but thank Him with your whole body, your whole mind, and your whole heart. Fill yourself up with the feeling of gratitude.

> *Philippians 4:11-12*
> 11*Not that* **I speak in respect of want**: *for I have learned, in whatsoever state I am,* therewith *to be content.*
> 12**I know both how to be abased, and I know how to abound**: *every where and in all things I am instructed both to be full and to be hungry, both to abound and to suffer need.*

BREATHING

Breathing through difficult times is required in the process of keeping your flesh in line. Breathing must be actively managed when you recognize a test. This can also be done during prayer and times of relaxation. Breathing properly, even in times of fight or flight, relaxes you so that you can better observe, hear instructions, and make decisions. A simple exercise is four seconds in and four seconds out. Practice this exercise until you can breathe for seven seconds in and out. Bringing the air, which is the Spirit, into the flesh tempers and levels your mind. God blew breath into Adam.

The air is a major part of our connection to the Most High. Air is our body's top priority even over food and water. Since we need air for a clear mind, this process of breathing is the first step every time you need to make a decision or take an action, even in fight or flight. This is not to be taken lightly or forgotten. Any time that your breathing is affected involuntarily, it is because of some type of fear or danger.

When under the duress of a test or temptation, also take these four breaths. If you can complete these four breaths, in or immediately after those four breaths you will have an opportunity to escape or find help. This is why it is always good to be near or in touch with people that can hold you accountable and assist and inspire you to walk upright. The first person of accountability for those that are married is their spouse. Do you have anyone in your life that is actively holding you accountable or makes you want to be better with just their presence?

Remember
More Promised
If something is taken from you, even your safety or livelihood, let it go. If you're moving properly and aligned with the Holy Spirit, room is being made for your next stage in life. John 10:11-18.

The Chase
What you are chasing is not happiness on Earth but eternal life thereafter.

Scale of Understanding
If you have the ability to properly observe something, you have a chance at understanding it. There are some things that can't be fully understood because we weren't there to observe the beginning process of them. Job 38:4.

Cleanliness
24 hour cycle reset to be back on track for the Kingdom. Leviticus 22:6-7 Psalm 30:5.

Above and Below
Everything is a macrocosm containing a microcosm. The beginning must be studied and then the end. Connect the dots from there. The Bible is no different. Do this with the New Testament and then the Old Testament. Read the end. Then read the beginning.

Physical Comfort
We have this incredible want for our flesh to be comfortable but making the flesh comfortable through vices will never do anything for your spirit. Get your spirit in-tune with the Comforter and everything else, including your flesh, will be comfortable. Notice, when your flesh is uncomfortable, it becomes stronger. Hold weight in your hands and your palms will callous. Your breathing will become difficult for a time but your cardiovascular system will gain capacity. The next day your flesh will be sore but soon your body will be able to hold more weight than it could before. Being uncomfortable

in the flesh makes your flesh strong enough to do the things requested of you by the Spirit. If this is what happens when your body is uncomfortable, imagine what happens when you make your mind uncomfortable. Now that you're strong physically and spiritually, go save a baby and don't forget to bring the milk. Matthew 6:33.

24
INTERMEDIUM

What should you do now? If you can't hear anything, there is a confusion between your internal voice and the voice of the Comforter. Maybe, you have not fully committed to being a child of the Most High. Is the Spirit bearing record? Read through the first 3 chapters of Proverbs and make sure that you understand the meaning of every word. Don't move on to the next word, scripture or chapter if you don't understand the current one.

For whatever reason, the Bible can sometimes seem difficult to read but it is your best friend. If it seems difficult, you're reading too much. Focus on each morsel. Read and meditate on a few scriptures or a chapter/section at a time. This isn't a reading contest to see how much you can read. This is a contest with yourself to make sure that you understand more today than you understood yesterday. That is what growth is about. The goal is to either have more understanding or a better understanding. Those are two different things. The words "more" and "better" are relative to your previous self and not someone else. This is an inward journey that is reflected externally.

Because you are not the only one on this journey of relationship with the Comforter, eventually, a new culture will emerge that is the same as the old. The original. What does a society governed by people who listen to the voice of the Most High look like?

The people with the most organization will be in control immediately. If organized crime will get you put out of your promised land, organized righteousness will get you put back in. Once this happens, the Most High will gather His people with the four winds. All paths of the strait and narrow lead here; to a joining of people sanctioned by the Most High God. The rest of the nations will follow like a moth to light.

If you are not of the people or a child of the Most High, the words in this book won't make much sense to you because this knowledge is sealed away from the children of the adversary. The next words are from the Most High.

> *Isaiah 28:23-26*
> *23***Give ye ear, and hear my voice***; hearken, and*
> ***hear my speech.***
> *24Doth the plowman plow all day to sow? doth he*
> *open and **break the clods of his ground?***
> *25When he hath made plain the face thereof, doth he*
> *not cast abroad the fitches, and scatter the*
> *cummin, and cast in the principal wheat and the*
> *appointed barley and the rie in their place?*
> *26**For his God doth instruct him to discre-***
> ***tion, and doth teach him.***

You are the ground work that is being prepared and the voice/speech/instruction is the seeds being scattered into the broken ground. The voice of the Comforter is the Most

High's voice which is sending the instruction deep into us, the broken fertile ground. We have to decide if we will no longer be thorny or hard ground.

This knowledge is not something that you should voluntarily share unless asked. It won't work for people who are operating in confusion and who are not of a pure heart. This understanding is only for those who seek it and ask of it.

The light is the Word. The light illuminates your path. The voice delivers the instructions that is the Word. You are the vessel that is the ultimate large language model (AI). In other words, you are the ultimate Word model.

> *Jeremiah 7:1 (partial)*
> *1 The **word that came** to Jeremiah **from the LORD**, saying,*

What is the word saying to you? The same way that the word of the Lord came to Jeremiah, it comes to you. Jeremiah is saying that the Voice of the Most High, that is the Holy Spirit, brought the Word of the Most High that is Christ.

Every second of your day is part of your journey, so naturally your journey is limited to how much time the Most High has gifted you with on Earth. If you drive where your eyes look, when your eyes are focused on the Most High that is where you will travel. The Most High desires the first of you and the most of you. Therefore, whoever can keep their eyes on Him first and the most will end where they need to be for the Most High. When you focus on distractions, that is where you will be led. The aim is to dedicate more and more of your seconds to Him out of each minute. Dedicate more minutes to Him out of each hour. Dedicate more days to Him out of each week. Dedicate more weeks to Him out of each month and so on. He has gifted us with time, so we need to give Him a tithe of our time. How do you give back to the

Most High to show your appreciation of the time He has gifted you with?

> *1 Chronicles 29:14*
> *14But who am I, and what is my people, that we should be able to offer so willingly after this sort? for all things come of thee, and of thine own have we given thee.*

As you are able to consistently keep your thoughts and mind focused on the Most High, this focus becomes your way. On this journey, the Most High will reward you according to your ways. This is the end of this writing, but it contains what can be considered to be the beginning of the way.

> *Psalm 25:1-4*
> *1{A Psalm of David.}*
> א
> *Unto thee, O LORD, do I lift up my soul.*
> ב
> *2O my God, I trust in thee: let me not be ashamed, let not mine enemies triumph over me.*
> ג
> *3Yea, let none that wait on thee be ashamed: let them be ashamed which transgress without cause.*
> ז
> *4Shew me thy ways, O LORD; teach me thy paths.*

Selah.

Appendix

All praises be to the Most High God in the name of the Son with the Holy Spirit, the Comforter.

Sacred Names Of God
I AM THAT I AM
IHVH; Derivatives - YEHOVAH, JEHOVAH, YAHAWAH, YAHUAH
ADNI; Derivatives - ADONAI, ADON, EDEN
IIAH; Derivatives - YIAI, YH, YAH, EHYEH
AHIH; Derivatives - EHYEH, AHAYAH

Sacred Names of the Son
YSH; Derivatives - YASHA, YASHAYA, YASHU, YASHUAH, YAHAWASHI, YHOWSHUWA, YEHOSHUA, JEHOSHUA, JESUS, IESOUS, IESOU

www.ingramcontent.com/pod-product-compliance
Lightning Source LLC
Chambersburg PA
CBHW030446100526
44580CB00001B/7